My family tree

Uncle

Aunt

Uncle

Cousins

Cousins

Cousins

What to Do When— And Why

Illustrated by Christiane

What to Do When— And Why

*At School, at Parties, at Home,
in Your Growing World*

Marjabelle Young Stewart
and
Ann Buchwald

LUCE

Robert B. Luce, Inc.
540 Barnum Avenue
Bridgeport, CT 06608

All handwriting samples are included from Renée C. Martin's *Scriptease* published by New Hope Publishing Company, Lahaska, Pennsylvania, at $1.50.)

Library of Congress Cataloging in Publication Data

Stewart, Marjabelle Young.
What to do when, and why.

SUMMARY: *Advises the pre-teen girl on manners,*
beauty care, being a likeable person, and generally
dealing with life's situations.
1. Etiquette for children and youth. [1. Etiquette.
2. Conduct of life. 3. Beauty, Personal. 4. Girls.]
I. Buchwald, Ann, joint author.
II. Title.
BJ1857.C5S82   395'.1'22   75-31840
ISBN 0-88331-105-4
Manufactured in the United States of America
Designed by The Etheredges

Dedicated to: Jackie, Maxine, Eleanore, Helene, Lora, Dorothy, Patt, Mitzi, Sue, Maeve, Elaine, Teresa, Joan, Jewel, Madeline, Jill, Thalia, Veda, Hildegarde, Blanca, Carole, Katherine, Ruth Ann, Jana, Bonnie, Eva, Margaret, Flora, Betsy, Alice, Barbara, Norma, Jan, Virginia, Edith, Henrietta, Elizabeth, Martha, Amy, Julie, Lillian, Marjorie, Millie, Judy, Sherie, Marcia, Beverly, Aranlie, Marita, and Dorise.

And especially to our young consultants:

Katherine Anthony
Cecilia Carter
Anne Fisher
Laura Newbern
Jill Richards
Marina Rust
    and particularly Joan Conway

THE AUTHORS

Contents

By Way
of
Introduction

Everyone needs help on the way up. Executives attend seminars to learn more advanced techniques so that they can become company presidents. Even teachers take refresher courses.

This book is for young people who are aware that not only their age category has changed—they're no longer little children—but that their minds and bodies are changing, too. Also, their goals, their dreams, even their fears.

How can you be sure and confident about yourself without always waiting for parents to show you the way? (Sometimes by a put-down instead of a lift *up!*)

One easy and useful way is to check yourself against some of the no-no's and right-on's of your special age, a period of years that is filled with confusion, but wonderful because this is the time of your life that determines the way you'll be as a teenager and young adult.

1

Manners Are Not Optional

If you want to live comfortably and peacefully with people, you need a few guidelines so that you won't feel awkward, shy, or nervous. Once you're sure of these universal practices, you can forget how and why you learned them and just have a good time.

Here's a before-and-after example:

THE OLD SELF-CONSCIOUS YOU

YOUR OLDER SISTER: "Who's your new friend?"
YOU: "That's Jimmy, dummy. Why are you so nosy?"
YOUR OLDER SISTER: "What's his last name?"
YOU: "How would *I* know?!?"

THE NEW SELF-CONFIDENT YOU

YOUR OLDER SISTER: "Who's your new friend?"
YOU: "This is Jimmy Banks from school. Jimmy, this is my sister Jane. Tell her about the poster we have to make."

Suddenly your sister is happy, you're happy, and the world looks pretty good because you know how to handle a situation smoothly. Whether it's picking up the right fork or knowing the proper way to greet a VIP, all manners make sense in themselves because they tell you what to do and what is expected of you. But the best part about manners is that they make you a nicer person to have around. If you've been ignoring good manners until now, or if people around you have been too busy to teach them, this book will help you find out what to do when—and why—as you gradually branch out from home base.

Making the Best of Your Inner Self

For almost as long as you can remember, your world has been your parents and family. Then whammo! Suddenly you discover there's a whole other world out there and it revolves around the friendships you make and keep. It's true that if you have two really good friends they're enough for a lifetime, but how does that miracle come about? It usually happens when you have the luxury of choosing from among many acquaintances.

HOW DO YOU BECOME A PERSON WITH MANY FRIENDS?

A person without pals will probably perform badly at school and be sulky at home. In fact, a person without one good friend may be a math genius but she'll still be a miserably lonely person.

No one hands you a perfectly made friendship. You have to BE friendly to make friends. It's not exactly work, but you have to earn popularity: be pleasant, look as if you enjoy life, think of others, and you'll be fun to be with.

Unless you're a dazzling beauty, or look like Robert Redford's kid sister, you'll often have to make the first step. Overcome your shyness—which is basically a fear that others won't like you—and say something, *anything* that seems reasonable: "Hi, were you caught in that traffic jam this morning, too?"

Friendships aren't built on happy talk alone. Sometimes a word of sympathy works wonders. Example: a girl blushes right down to her sneakers when she gives the wrong answer in class. You can say, "I know just how you felt. Don't you wish there were anti-blush pills?"

Sometimes a new friend is acquired by way of generosity on your part. Example: she's just won the decisive point in a game or the lead role in the play. Tell her she's terrific or that she saved the day. At that moment you become her umbrella against a torrent of envy or jealous, snide remarks.

IF YOU DON'T HAVE ENOUGH FRIENDS

If you don't have enough friends or if you're not getting along with the ones you have, maybe you're doing something wrong and don't realize it. Here are some questions to ask yourself privately and honestly, knowing each and all of these situations can be corrected once you recognize them.

Are you deliberately looking for trouble?

Do you imagine that others are out to slight or insult you, when on second thought it could be that they're busy, worried, or in a jam you couldn't possibly know about? No one, not even your mother, thinks about you twenty-four hours a day. If you think your feelings should be uppermost in your friends' lives, you'll become egotistic, and, of course, disappointed at least once a day.

Are you a put-downer?

Friendships can be broken forever, or certainly bent out of shape, by a sarcastic put-down. Insecure people use sarcasm to belittle those who seem confident and sure of themselves. The best antidote to sarcasm, when you're on the receiving end, is a good laugh! Try it—the next time someone makes fun of you, be the first to laugh. In a split second you suddenly become a good sport instead of a dum-dum.

Are you a gossip?

Worse yet is a vicious gossip. Gossip is basically naughty news and you know it, otherwise you wouldn't be whispering when there's no one around for miles except the person you're whispering to. When you gossip, you play dirty pool in order to seem better than the person you're gossiping about. The worst form is the direct quote of an insult: "Sue said you're the biggest liar she's ever met," or "Sue really hates you but she told me not to tell you."

Sometimes classmates will walk away when you try to defend someone they're gossiping about, but try anyway. Look for something good in the person or the situation —you'll always find it.

Are you a bowl of jealousy?

It will show, you know. Envy sticks out like an acne pimple. If your stomach churns with envy, stop and realize that no one has everything she wants in the world. You may think so, but negatives are always there, even though you may not be able to see them. Just as positives are there in you. Look for them in yourself, write them down—the things you do best and the personal qualities you're secretly proud of—find a way to bring them out in the open, and the old green-eyed monster will crawl away. It's vital to do this now, because you'll find that even the most successful person is uneasy around jealous people who seem to be lying in wait for a mistake, ready to pounce, watching too closely for comfort. Looking up to a person, even hero-worshipping, is different. Everyone loves an appreciative friend, but a jealous one is always a threat.

Do you throw a fit when you don't get your way?

Your opinions could be 100 percent right, but if you have a tantrum the minute you're crossed, your friends will soon be disgusted—and absent. It's OK, though, to flare up when you see unfairness or mistreatment of people; that kind of anger shows you care and that you're sure enough of your principles to speak out and defend them.

Are you too possessive?

Cherish your record player, your 10-speed bike, even your stuffed animal collection—but don't consider your friends *things* to possess and never to be shared. When your closest friend goes to a movie with someone else, she is not deserting you—she is merely widening her circle. She can still be your most confidential pal, providing you trust her to do a few things you're not in on.

Sometimes three people can be a close trio, but it's rare. It takes delicate tuning to keep all three people on the same wavelength. Usually, when the going gets tough, two will gang up on the third. So for the time being stick to twos, fours, or sixes.

Are you too aggressive?

Congratulations, you're a born leader and you know it. But if your friends call you bossy, pushy, or loud you'll be leading an army of one. Original ideas and the determination to put them over are as valuable as being born with perfect pitch, but plain old bulldozing alienates friends because you're telling them their ideas don't count. Therefore you're really telling them that they don't count either.

Do you punish your friends when you've had a hard knock?

You get a perfectly innocent call from your school friend after dinner, and because your parents have found out about your one failing grade, you scream, "I hate that teacher, I hate that school, and I hate you, too, for that matter!" Take the hard knocks alone, or share them—but don't transfer them.

Are you a poor sport?

We're not talking about Olympics here, we're talking about playing fair—whether it's a game or a competition or a struggle for popularity or good grades. You either play fair or you don't, and your friends find this out sooner or later. Be quick to congratulate a winner, or at least try to smile when you lose. Win or lose by the rules. Don't blame losing on your allergies, the coach, the teacher, or your stupid younger sister.

Are you a troublemaker?

If even the most innocent arguments somehow end up in harsh words, ask yourself if you're the one who starts the trouble. People should be able to try their ideas out on each other. If you want to be a real friend, remember how important it is to *listen*—to even the farthest-out opinions. If you insist on the last word, claim that yours is the only logical conclusion, your friends will take their ideas elsewhere.

To avoid unnecessary arguments, avoid subjects you know will explode—race, religious viewpoints, even politics if you've found in the past that the mere mention of that person or issue has caused a fight. Some statements "set fires"—they bring out the worst in people. When you know it and still bring up the subject purely for the pleasure of seeing people tear into each other, you're a troublemaker. Is that really the kind of person you want to be?

If you find yourself in an argument, here are ways to minimize the antagonism:

* KEEP YOUR VOICE PLEASANT. The louder a person argues, the less convincing she or he is. People listen better to a voice that isn't strained, loud, or full of superiority and disgust.

* LISTEN TO OTHERS WITH AN OPEN MIND. Your own opinion may not change, but you could pick up an additional and useful twist.

* CHANGE THE SUBJECT WHEN YOU SENSE THE APPROACH OF VIOLENT WORDS OR ACTIONS. Don't apologize or explain, just quickly introduce another topic: "Who wants to go bike riding Sunday?" Anything for cooling-off time.

Do you serve sour grapes?

"No wonder she won, she blah, blah, blah," or "I

9

wouldn't count on her, she never keeps her word," or simply, "You *like* her?!?" Remember that nobody willingly swallows two sour grapes in a row.

Can you say you're sorry when you are?

Even the toughest hold-out will give in when you say, "I'm sorry for what I said (or did). I was wrong; can you forgive me?" And when you have been wronged, can you stand there and gracefully accept another person's apology? If you can't forget the whole thing, at least shove it to the back of your mind and get on with life.

Are you your own worst critic?

Do you constantly put yourself down or deny the good things people say to you: "Oh, this old skirt! My sister gave it to me because she hated it!" or "I know I'll never get a good part in the play," or "Who'd invite *me?*" or "No sense in my trying; I never win anything!"? These are danger signals that let you know that you are too self-critical. People feel like shaking you, but you're the only one who can shake off those feelings of low esteem. If you need help about a poor self-image, ask for it from an older member of your family, your school advisor, a minister, or a doctor. Talk honestly about each inferior feeling you have, taking them one by one until you've replaced them with more positive and realistic ones.

Do your friends have to be perfect?

Your friend has just done a stupid thing: "Wow, I always thought you were smarter than *that!*" Or she has one disappointing weakness—she breaks things, loses things, is late a lot. Do you erase her from your slate? The odds are you can't completely change her, but you *can* talk calmly with her about why she does what she does and you can try to understand it. Nobody's perfect, but you can like a person in spite of her failings once you see them clearly.

Are you letting a group do your dirty work for you?

There's always one group that waits for the rules to be posted so they'll know what they WON'T do. Even if they hate school and see a sign saying "school closed today —no one allowed in" they'd find a way to crawl in through the basement. Basically, those in that group want to be noticed even if it means getting punished. Eventually it's this same group that gets into trouble with drugs, petty theft, the police. If you feel like rebelling at times—and who doesn't?—rebel on your own with your eyes open, but don't make the group the heavy.

Some Problems Can't Be Helped by Band Aids

You're shy

Your parents try to help by explaining, "She's always been shy," and that only makes it worse. You begin to think there's something wrong with you. But shyness denotes a particular temperament, that's all. There's nothing abnormal about being shy; some people adapt more easily and quickly than others. A shy person is actually a lot more comfortable to be with than a gangbuster type who is always "on." And shy people, because they take their time, often make deeper and more lasting friendships than the hyped-up personalities do. Shy people are simply more sensitive to others, and often become great artists, musicians, writers, or thinkers. If it's difficult for you to start a conversation, try these two devices:

1. Ask someone for advice . . . about a homework problem, the rules of a new game, how to get somewhere. Everyone likes being needed and the chances are that

from one little question you'll have the beginnings of a friendship.

2. Offer to help someone . . . with an assignment, a ride home, a heavy load of books or supplies, the simple loan of a dime to make a phone call.

You don't want to be a tomboy anymore

But you're afraid to be called a prissy. It's a strain to strut and show off, act tough all the time, put every boy down, yet you're fearful of being alienated from the group. Maybe you'd like to walk home with a boy who lives near you; maybe you'd like to walk home alone. Do so and think your own thoughts, realizing that girls who dictate strict rules, then bully everyone into obeying them, are merely covering up their own insecurity. They haven't quite decided what kind of girl they want to be—but you have!

You feel you're on the outside, looking in

It's more fun to be in the center of the action. The best way is to join as many groups, clubs, school activities, teams—sports, scouting, drama, dance, photography, ceramics—as you can honestly contribute to. Try them one at a time until you figure out the ones that make you happy. At least one person in each group will have joined for the same reason and you'll soon locate each other. Warning: a sure way to stay on the sidelines watching others having fun is to pooh-pooh or ridicule a group you haven't been invited to join, or to say, "Who wants to learn about messy old ceramics?" or "Who cares? That's for babies anyway."

You had a good friend and you lost her

Not to a stranger, but to another good friend; now they're *best* friends. It can happen, and you feel cheated. Maybe it was jealousy, your possessiveness, or out-and-out manipulation by the third person. Best solution: get together and say, "Let's straighten this out. I like you both and we all like each other, so why can't we stop the contest? Three's only a crowd on a date!" It may be a difficult step but it's easier than crying yourself to sleep.

You had a good friend and you lost him

Someone stole your boyfriend and it really hurts, especially during pre-teen years when boy–girl friendships are iffy from the start. First you had to go along with the group and say all boys were yukky, then you worked up the courage to admit you'd found one boy who wasn't *too* awful, and finally you realized he liked you enough to show it by such tender gestures as tripping you in the hall or offering to Indian wrestle with you. Now someone else has run off with your status symbol. The best plan is to wait it out, smile, and say so long for now. Don't try to talk him out of it—he'll feel hassled, guilty, indispensable, or all three things. If he really likes you, he'll come around again. If not, keep your eyes open for someone else you feel good with.

You have gigantic hassles about homework and obligations

You like your mother to remind you of reports due in two weeks. You appreciate a little help looking up special things in the encyclopedia. And you certainly need a lift to the public library at times. But the conflict comes when all TV is banned until homework is finished. Maybe it's because your parents feel that your favorite TV programs are junk; maybe they are afraid commercials tempt you into buying too many faulty gadgets with your precious allowance. Talk it over with your parents; stage "Let's Make a Deal" right in your own living room. Discuss the shows you really hate to give up versus the ones you're willing to compromise on. Make a deal about the hours you'll spend on homework and reading or hobbies. When you show how responsible you can be, your parents will stop peering at you to see if you're turning into a zombie.

Here are two ways to show that you are responsible:

* PUT A BULLETIN BOARD IN YOUR ROOM and tack up reminders of school reports due, doctors' appointments, piano or dancing classes, planned family trips. Then you

won't be surprised or angry when they happen and you have to cancel something that's more fun to do.

* KEEP AN ADDRESS BOOK OF YOUR OWN for the telephone numbers and addresses of friends you call most often, for doctors, dentists, special teachers you have regular appointments with. That way, in case you have to cancel or change a date, or have to get ther alone by bus or taxi in an emergency, you'll have all the facts at hand. Don't forget to add your father's office phone and address—and your mother's, too, if she has a job outside the home.

You have a hunch the teacher dislikes you

If it's your homeroom teacher, your life can be miserable. You can tremble with dread every morning and plan to run away if things don't improve, or you can be sensible.

It's either imaginary or real. It's imaginary if you're striving for preferential treatment and are not getting it, or if your teacher said on the first day, "I hope you're as good a student as that wonderful big brother of yours was!" and you're setting a goal no one, not even your brother, has asked you to top. If you're old enough to feel bad vibes, you're perfectly adequate to figure out that maybe the teacher is having trouble at home (most of them are married these days and have children and houses to worry about), is in bad health, is new at the school or in the course she's teaching. Then talk it over with your parents. Do everything you can to make the situation work out before you write her off as an enemy; otherwise your work and attention in her class will be the losers.

It could be real if you're not leveling with yourself about bugging the teacher, being sarcastic, supplying alibis instead of finished homework, or making fun of the teacher just loudly or closely enough for her to hear or see. Maybe you just haven't learned how to deal with authority; now's a good time to learn this important skill. Shape up.

SHOW THIS TO YOUR PARENTS

Some TV shows you think of as junk are not so in the minds of teenagers and pre-teenagers. Fantasy, escape, and science fiction programs don't necessarily remove a young person from reality but often help her/him relate to it.

Watch a few of your daughter's or son's favorite shows with her/him, talk about them during commercial breaks, and you may find that those shows are supplying missing elements in their lives, or are actually helping them to think about a problem they couldn't express without a little help from the fictionalized version on the tube.

About hard-sell commercials? Ask them what they think and you will be amazed at how quickly 9- to 12-year-olds see through phoniness and unbelievable claims. They might even educate you about some of the products you fell for!

Things No Mirror Will Tell You

You've heard people say, "I love her, warts and all," and it could be true. But here is a list of invisible uglies that no one likes in others. If you have any of these, remove them:

AFFECTATION—putting on airs.

INSINCERITY—not meaning what you say in the slightest; also known as buttering-up when it's a false compliment to a teacher or a flattering remark to someone from whom you want a favor.

NAME-DROPPING—"Guess what Paul said to my father last night on the phone!" "Paul who?" "Paul-Robinson-the-mayor, dummy!"

BEING SHOW-OFF UNFEMININE—deliberately acting tomboyish, with dirty fingernails, sloppy hair, and torn shirt.

CONCEIT—mirror, mirror on the wall, on the stairs, in every doorway, showing you think you are indeed the prettiest and most talented of them all. Too much of that and the only friendly face you'll find is in your own looking glass.

THOUGHTLESSNESS—pushing, whispering in front of some-one, giggling and pointing, laughing at someone's mistake or bad luck.

SELFISHNESS—being so spoiled you refuse to share; always wanting the first, best, most; being greedy whether it's for the front seat in the car or the whole candy bar.

FLIRTING WITH SOMEONE ELSE'S BOYFRIEND—you may win him over, but you'll lose her as a friend, so you're back to Start. What's the gain? Find your own boyfriend or wait until hers is on his own.

ROUGH LANGUAGE—as the backbone of a vocabulary. Every-body likes to let off steam by exploding with a few hot swear words now and then—besides, it gives you a temporary sense of being ten feet tall—but if you use such language day in and day out your friends will be afraid to have you around, especially in their homes.

Too Fat,
Too Thin, Too Short,
Too Tall

You look in a mirror and get a shock because for a little while you forgot what you look like. Have you ever stood in front of a mirror with your face close to the glass and stared at yourself for a long time as if at a stranger? If you have you know how unreal and distorted you look. However, it *is* a good idea to glance at yourself every single day—not too intensely nor too long—just to check up on your appearance and the changes that are occurring. Many times you feel you're not shaping up fast enough or in the right spots. That's because you're trying to get the whole picture of yourself from a mirror only, when what you must also look for is a sense of your own identity.

A sense of identity is a feeling everyone aims for—a sense of place within your own family, a sense of place that makes you feel comfortable with your own circle of friends. Every bit of growing up and developing—figuring out who and what you are—is so gradual and seems to take such a long time that you could become impatient to get it over with. But it's the gradual pace that does you the most good. Otherwise you'd suffer from the sudden change and be exhausted trying to catch up with your own metamorphosis.

Your Outward Self –
How to
Beautify It

It's difficult to get straight answers from your family when you first begin to wonder how to make yourself prettier or how to analyze your best points versus your weaker ones. Your mother and father will tell you you're "fine just the way you are," but that's not what you're looking for.

This is the time to take stock of how you look, walk, stand, wear your hair, and appear to others. And there are definite guide posts to help you.

YOUR POSTURE IS THE SELF-PORTRAIT OF YOU THAT OTHERS SEE FIRST

Without realizing it, you may have let bad posture take over. Perhaps you have developed *hunched shoulders* because you feel you're too tall. Or a *sway-back* because you've neglected to tuck in your fanny all these years of living in jeans. Or a *lazy, lumpy waistline* from slouching at school or slumping in front of the TV. Perhaps you've just let your

22

non-flat tummy stick out because you figure it doesn't show with loose sweaters and shirts. Whatever the reasons, start now to correct your posture and improve your fast-growing figure. Your clothes will look better, you'll become more attractive, and your backbone will have a chance to grow straight again.

Here are the posture no-no's to check yourself against:

* Is your head thrust forward on your shoulders as if you're Sherlock Holmes hunting for clues?

* Are your shoulders hunched forward? (This is the "poor-little-me, no-one-cares" look)

* Does your chest cave in?

* Does your tummy protrude; is it farther out than your chest?

* Does your fanny stick out too far?

* Do your knees look too straight and stiff?

* Do your feet point outward, duck fashion?

Find out how good posture feels

Stand with your back to the wall, feet about two inches from the base of the wall, back touching the wall, arms straight at sides, head and shoulders back. Slowly bend your knees and slide down the wall to a sitting position. Hold, then push your body up the wall with every point of your spine touching the wall.

Concentrate on tensing your buttocks, keeping your hips tucked under, and pressing the small of your back to the wall. Start by doing this 4 times and then gradually increase to 15 times daily.

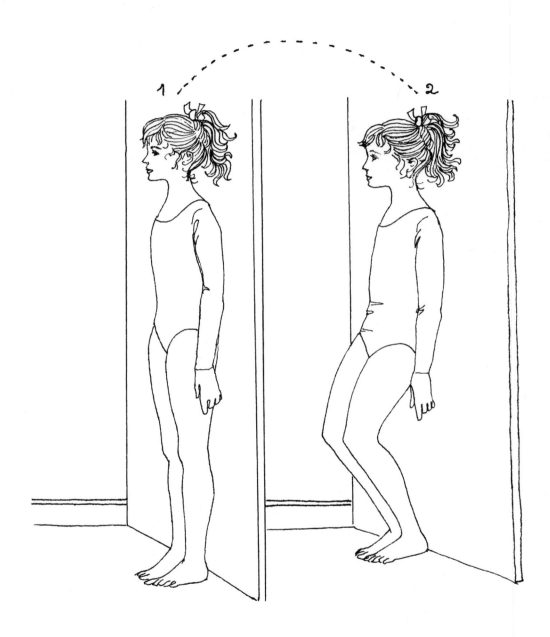

An easy and sure-fire exercise to correct poor posture

Stand in your bare feet facing a wall. Place palms flat against the wall.

Bend your arms until chin and elbows are touching the wall. Keep feet flat on the floor. Bend at ankles only; keep your knees straight.

Straighten arms, push away from the wall. Hold head high, keep feet firmly on the floor. Repeat 10 times.

FIGURE OUT WHERE YOU ARE AND WHERE YOU WANT TO BE

YOUR AGE	YOUR HEIGHT	YOUR WEIGHT SHOULD BE
9 to 10 years	52″ to 55″	64 to 71 pounds
11 to 12 years	55″ to 60″	71 to 95 pounds
13 to 14 years	60″ to 63″	95 to 113 pounds

How do you measure up?

Here are some standard measurements you can use as a guide to planning a few goals during the next few months:

HEIGHT	5′ to 5′3″	5′4″ to 5′7″	5′8″ to 6′
BUST	33″ to 34″	35″ to 36″	36½″ to 38″
WAIST	10 inches less than bust		
HIPS	33″ to 34″	35″ to 36″	36½″ to 38″
THIGH	17″ to 18″	18½″ to 20″	20½″ to 21½″
CALF	12″ to 13″	13″ to 14″	13½″ to 14½″
ANKLE	6½″ to 7″	7″ to 7¾″	7¾″ to 8″

Present Date _____

BUST _____

WAIST _____

HIPS _____

THIGH _____

CALF _____

ANKLE _____

WEIGHT _____

Goal Date
Six months from present _____

BUST _____

WAIST _____

HIPS _____

THIGH _____

CALF _____

ANKLE _____

WEIGHT _____

EASY EXERCISES
FOR SPECIFIC TROUBLE SPOTS

To correct a forward-thrust head

Stand with feet about 18 inches apart, hands resting on backs of thighs. Now bend head and spine as far back as you can; try to see the wall behind you. Repeat 5 times daily.

For a flatter tummy

Lie on your back on the floor. With legs straight, feet together, raise legs several inches from the floor. Count to 5 while holding legs up. Lower legs. Repeat 5 times.

For slimmer hips

Sit on the floor with legs straight out in front of you. Stretch first your right, then left heel as far ahead as you can, edging your hips forward on the floor at the same time. Balance with your arms straight out in front of you. "Crawl" across your bedroom floor and back once every morning, once every night, and your extra inches around the hips will soon disappear.

For a slimmer waistline

Kneel on the floor with arms outstretched at shoulders. Swing upper body to left, then to right, twisting hard. Repeat 10 times.

For slimmer calves

Stand with toes on edge of a book, barefoot. Let heels down as far as possible, then lift up on toes. You'll feel a pull which will streamline "fatted calves."

For more shapely thighs

Kneel on the floor, legs slightly apart, arms folded on chest. Keeping your head, spine, and legs in a straight line, lean back slowly till you feel a pull on thigh muscles. Return slowly to upright position. Repeat 10 times.

To develop a pretty bust

Stand upright; clasp hands in front of your chest, elbows pointed to sides. Press palms together and hold for a count of 5. Relax; repeat 10 times.

GOOD LOOKS BEGIN WITH A GOOD DIET

Sure, you could live forever on bologna sandwiches and peanut butter, but to have a clear complexion, healthy nails and bones, and shining hair, you're going to need more than fun foods. Here are the basics you must start including in your daily eating:

PROTEIN—three servings daily of any meat, poultry, fish, eggs, cheese, milk, soybeans, or nuts. A lack of protein causes muscles to grow flabby and lazy, peeling or broken fingernails, and dull hair.

VEGETABLES—two servings daily of green vegetables, leafy salads, and yellow vegetables like carrots and squash. They're the secret of curing skin problems.

WHOLE-GRAIN CEREALS OR BREAD—at least one serving a day. They contain Vitamin E, which is known as the "hair vitamin." Seeds like pumpkin and sunflower are also rich in Vitamin E.

FRUITS OR FRUIT JUICES—at least one serving a day for the Vitamin C they contain. Citrus fruits, tomatoes, strawberries, and cantaloupe are very good.

MILK—whether whole or skimmed, depending on your weight problem, essential for straight bones, shiny, fastgrowing hair, and pretty fingernails because all milk is rich in calcium.

WATER—doctors would like you to drink at least four glasses a day, and if you start gulping now you'll have less acne during teen years.

FATS—believe it or not, your body needs oils and fats such as butter, cream, and oil to help "burn" protein so the body can use it properly.

If you wonder how many of the above foods to eat in order to be healthy but never overweight, study these calorie charts:

SMART GIRL SNACKS	Calories
Celery, 1 stalk	5
Lettuce, ¼ head	15
Strawberries, ¼ cup	15
Carrot, 1 whole	20
Pretzels, 5 small	20
Grapefruit, ½	25
Cucumber slices, about 30	25
Gingersnap cookie, 1	25
Tomato, 1 small	25
Apple, ½ medium	40

SO-SO SNACKS	Calories
Grape juice, ½ cup	80
Banana	85
Corn on cob, 1	85
Brownie, 1 large	100
Cheese, 1½" cube (1 ounce)	100
Cornflakes, ¾ cup	100
Raisins, ¼ cup	115
Watermelon (1 slice)	115
Peanuts, 20	115

WEIGHT WRECKERS	Calories		Calories
Sweet roll	135	10¢ candy bar	335
Hotdog	155	Apple pie, 1 slice	345
Bun	100	Popcorn, 1 box	350
Soft drinks, 2 glasses	160	Pizza, 2 slices	370
Hamburger, broiled	185	Chocolate sundae	375
Jelly doughnut	220	Malt with ice cream	485
Ice cream soda	255	Banana Split	820

ARE YOU BOTHERED BY A SPECIAL BEAUTY PROBLEM?

Icky hair, fingernails that peel or break?

More protein and calcium are needed: milk, cottage cheese, meat, fish, nuts, yeast. Hair experts say hair is made up of 90 percent protein.

Very dry skin or beginning of acne break-outs?

More Vitamin A is needed: leafy green vegetables, salads, liver, egg yolks, apricots, yellow vegetables.

Permanent "goose pimples"

On thighs and upper arms? More Vitamin A is needed (see vitamin list).

Frequent colds, bruises from the slightest bumps?

More Vitamin C is needed: found in all citrus fruits, green peppers, cauliflower, cabbage, kale, tomatoes, all berries.

Dry lips, "loose hair" (too much comes out on hairbrush at each brushing)?

More Vitamin B-2 is needed: found in milk, cheeses, eggs, cereal, and grains.

Poor, sickly coloring? No-glow complexion?

More Vitamin E is needed: found in fish oils, wheat germ, eggs. You may also need Vitamin D, which is found mostly in good old sunshine—which you don't even have to look for! In fact, your body manufactures Vitamin D while you're sitting in the sun. Also found in milk, liver, and fish oils such as cod liver oil.

Unhealthy gums or spotty tooth enamel (even when you brush often and well)?

More Vitamin C is needed (see vitamin list).

Early-age insomnia?

More Vitamin B-6 is needed: found in wheat germ, egg yolks, and, of all things, cabbage.

A "not with it" feeling (unsteady nerves, low morale)?

More Vitamin B will help: found in whole wheat, corn, rice, oats, pork, asparagus.

INSIDE TIP—Going long periods without enough sleep can be disastrous for a pretty skin, just as lack of fresh air can make skin look dull. Do deep-breathing exercises at the window each morning, or go for a quick bike ride or a round of jogging. Your skin will glow.

SECOND LOOKS: THE SHAPE OF YOUR FACE AND THE RIGHT HAIR STYLE

If your face is OVAL-SHAPED, with wide cheekbones, narrow at chin and forehead:
Wear your hair with a low side part, letting hair fall forward on cheeks to minimize width.
Avoid skinning your hair back tightly or hiding that desirable oval shape behind a lot of fussiness and curls.

If your face is HEART-SHAPED, with wide forehead, width at cheeks, a narrow jawline, almost a pointed chin:
Wear your hair in an asymmetrical (off-side) line, smooth, and with hair coming forward toward cheeks.
Avoid wearing your hair flat on top or skinned back.

If your face is TRIANGLE-SHAPED *(often called pear-shaped)*, narrow at forehead and wide at cheeks, then narrow again at jawline and chin:

Wear your hair fairly short with height at center of head, close at sides.

Avoid adding width to the sides of your face. Flatness on top will just exaggerate the width of your cheeks; so will ear-length flips of hair.

If your face is ROUND, with a broad forehead, wide cheekbones, and a rounded and wide jawline:

Wear your hair high on top, starting with low side part; bring hair forward toward cheeks.

Avoid bangs or flat-on-top hairstyles, or long hair with flip below jawline.

If your face is LONG, with forehead, cheeks, and jaw all on the same line approximately, but longer than wide:

Wear your hair with a soft effect at the forehead, smooth curls toward cheekbones to break the long line.

Avoid severe, long, straight styles or any pulled-back line.

GIVE YOUR SKIN WHAT IT WANTS

If your skin is NORMAL, neither greasy nor dry in appearance; with a fine and even texture; pink or glowing with color (lucky you!):

CLEANSE
Use mild soap and water 3 times a day.

FRESHEN
Splash on cool water or freshener after each washing. Then, for circulation, pat face briskly until it tingles.

PAMPER
Use a little moisturizing lotion (baby lotion if you wish) after A.M. cleansing; a little cream before bed.

If your skin is DRY, rough, scaly; feels tight or drawn:

CLEANSE
Gently with castile soap and warm water; or with cleansing cream followed by warm water.

FRESHEN
Splash with cold water. Pat dry quickly. Avoid letting water dry on skin.

PAMPER
Use baby lotion or moisturizing lotion after each washing. Increase your intake of butter, cream, and salad oils.

If your skin is OILY, with an oily sheen most of the time; enlarged pores, blackheads, or pimples:

CLEANSE
Use cleansing lotion or medicated soap 3 times a day; rinse well. Instead of a washcloth, use a complexion brush for better, deeper cleansing.

FRESHEN
With an astringent after each washing.

PAMPER
Avoid fried foods. Wash scalp, hairline, face, and shoulders often. Get more sunshine.

34

If you have PROBLEM SKIN:

SENSITIVE SKIN
Usually it is also dry
skin; follow routine
for dry.

BLACKHEADS
Steam your face with
hot washcloth, then
apply a special pore
mask; or if you do it
carefully, squeeze out
blackheads using
tissues wrapped
around fingers to
avoid red marks.

ACNE
Use medicated soap
twice a day with a soft
facial brush; rinse
both your face *and*
your facial brush lav-
ishly.

If you have COMBINATION SKIN; oily around the "T"-Zone
but dry outside the T-Zone areas:

You must follow directions for both DRY and OILY skin
where they apply. Remember that the oily parts of your skin
collect all the dust and dirt in the air, creating large pores
and blackheads; so pay special attention to these, using a
bacteria-fighting soap or lotion if necessary.

FACIALS ARE NO BIG DEALS

They're easy, fun, and they pay off in glowing complexions.
Here are the six easy steps to follow:

1. First, tie back your hair and remove clothing and
   jewelry from around your neck and shoulders.
2. Remove dirt, grime, or any make-up from face and
   neck until washcloth is clean.
3. Steam your skin to open pores. Hold your face over a
   basin of hot running water with a towel-tent over your
   head until steam makes droplets of water plip-plop
   into the basin. Takes 5 minutes.

4. Clean skin again with soap and water or a cleansing lotion, paying special attention to the T-Zone—center of forehead, nose, chin.
5. Splash with cool water. Rinse thoroughly.
6. Blot face dry.

Apply either of these two masques to tighten pores, refine your skin, and give your face a gorgeous glow.

Honey facial for normal skin

You'll need face cream (Nivea or Vaseline will do), a tablespoon of honey, some ice water, and a freshener. After regular cleansing, massage your face with the cream. Then remove cream and pat on honey (gently around the eye area and more briskly around face planes and neck). Press your fingers on your face and pull away quickly, using the stickiness of the honey to stimulate your skin's circulation. Continue for 2–3 minutes. Press a warm towel (wrung out in hot water) over your face to remove the honey. Rinse out and press towel three times to steam face, then follow with another towel dipped in ice water. Pat your face dry with a soft towel.

Epsom salt facial for oily skin

You'll need a cup of hot water, epsom salts, and cotton pads. After regular cleansing of your face, dissolve one heaping tablespoon of epsom salts thoroughly in a cup of hot water. Pat solution over face using cotton pads. Repeat twice. Then sponge off with cold water. Pat your face dry with a soft towel.

OTHER COMPLEXION PROBLEMS

MOLES. Do not molest. Usually they can be surgically removed by a doctor, or perhaps accented as a beauty mark.

FRECKLES. The pet hate of most girls, though they have been voted as very attractive (by those who don't have them!). They can be prevented in part by staying out of the sun, or wearing a big hat and a sun-screen cream or lotion during the summer. Later on, when you're older and wearing make-up, a cream foundation will hide them almost entirely.

SCARS. Plastic surgeons can now make even the worst scars disappear, but you have to be at least 16 years old before you undergo this type of surgery; otherwise scars may reappear as you continue to grow. Meanwhile, there are excellent "cover-up sticks" in all drugstores to hide scars.

BIRTHMARKS. Once again, cover-up sticks and foundations can do a lot to camouflage birthmark discolorations. But don't let minor ones spoil your good times, good looks, or good disposition. Your personality is much more important than any other factor in your life.

BLACKHEADS. Can be squeezed out with your fingertips after first cleansing your face and steaming it with hot towels to open the pores. Wrap facial tissues around your fingers and work gently. Later on, you can buy a dome extractor at any drugstore. This is a small device which lifts out blackheads by suction. Always apply a good astringent or witch hazel after either method of removing blackheads. Beware of spreading infection by picking at your face or overdoing blackhead squeezing.

SUNTANNING TO PERFECTION

You've heard plenty about the dangers of too much sun too fast—the risk of skin cancer and permanent freckles—yet it's still fun to get a pretty tan. It's like finding a new personality—you feel more confident and attractive—and a tan makes teeth look whiter, eyes brighter, hair blonder. Here's the way to get the most enviable tan:

* Before you go into the sun, apply suntan lotion—with a sun screen in it if you are very fair or delicate-skinned. If you have dark skin, use oil; even coconut or baby oil will do.

* Apply a nose-protector cream, stick, or gel.

* Put cotton pads dipped in water over your eyes. Sunglasses do not filter out bright sun rays which will make your eyes hurt.

* Apply a lip protector—Chap Stick will do.

* Lie down in the sun with an oven timer set for 5 to 20 minutes, depending on your skin type and the number of times you've been out in the first summer sun.

* When the timer goes off, splash your face with cool water and apply more suntan lotion. If you have sensitive skin, take a cool shower to reduce skin temperature; then wait 20 minutes before going back into the sun.

* If you do get sunburned, make a pitcher of very strong tea. Allow it to cool. Dip a face cloth or towel in the tea and place it over the burned area. You can put cooled tea bags on your closed eyelids if they get sunburned.

MMMMMM . . . WHAT A YUMMY BATH

Science now says an evening bath is better than a morning one. Much of your skin's natural pH barrier is removed by bathing; so if you take your bath at night, your skin has a whole night to replenish this natural protective coating.

If you have dry skin, put a tablespoon or two of baby oil or bath oil in the water. Prolonged soaking is not good—it takes too much moisture out of your skin. About 10 or 15 minutes is perfect. You have 15,000 square inches of skin on your body and it is constantly being "worn off" and renewed. Washing and rubbing with a washcloth helps this process, so a bath is not just for beauty but for health, too.

Before you begin your bath, collect the things you'll need. Make yourself a Beauty Box—just any box you've covered in pretty plastic paper to keep your personal grooming items in. You should have your shampoo, hair rinse, and the items you need for manicure and pedicure —an orange stick, emery board, nail brush, pumice stone, old toothbrush, bath brush, bath softener (try ¼ cup of oatmeal or 1 cup cornstarch tied in the toe of a nylon stocking).

Rub body oil all over your body, or swish your oatmeal or cornstarch stocking around in the tub to soften the water. Soak for 10 minutes.

Do part of your manicure and pedicure in the tub (the hot water will soften cuticles). Brush eyebrows with the old toothbrush—first up, then backward, then back the way they grow. Now use a good brush or your water-softening nylon stocking bag and clean your entire body, starting with your face. To clean your face, make a lather in your hands and go over your entire face, using circular motions with the pads of your fingertips.

Use your nail brush and pumice stone to smooth elbows, knees, heels, and knuckles. Natural bristles are kindest to skin and nails. While you're still in the tub moisten pumice stone and rotate it over rough spots, even the soles of your feet—especially during the summer when you go barefoot so much of the time. If you have dark spots on your elbows, rub them with a slice of lemon. Or, after your bath is finished, you can use an old trick: rest each elbow in half a grapefruit—one that has been eaten, of course—for 15 minutes.

LEARN TO GIVE YOURSELF A MANICURE

If your fingernails are snagged and bitten, your cuticles ragged, take a few minutes each week to give yourself a manicure. Soak your nails (if you haven't already done so in your bath) in warm water. Then:

* Remove any old polish.

* File your nails with an emery board—it's easier on the nails than a metal file. File in one direction only, from the side to the center. Avoid filing too low at the sides because that will weaken your nails and they'll break more often. All fingernails should be about the same length unless you want to look like a Mandarin with one long talon-nail.

* Soak nails in warm soapy water. If you wish to do this part in the bathtub, remember to file nails beforehand. It's difficult to file nails right after a hot bath—they're too soft. Clean nails with nail brush while they're soaking.

* Push cuticles back. This can be done partially with the towel as you dry your hands.

* Apply cuticle remover. Use an orange stick wrapped in cotton if there isn't a brush in the bottle.

* Loosen and remove dead cuticle with the flat end of the orange stick.

* Trim any hangnails. Don't make a habit of cutting cuticle; it will just grow tougher.

* Wash off cuticle remover with soapy water.

* Massage hands and arms with hand lotion right up to and including your elbows.

* Remove all traces of lotion or oil on nails with polish remover.

* Apply base coat, polish, and top coat. Remove a hairline from the tip of each nail to prevent polish from chipping. Do this with the thumb of the opposite hand as each fingernail is polished. If polish is allowed to dry even halfway it will ripple as you make the hairline.

You can improve the shape of your fingernails with colored polish:

A splay-shaped nail can be disguised to look oval.

A broad fingernail can look less so if only the middle is polished.

A long, narrow nail will look more oval if the moon section is left unpainted.

LEARN TO GIVE YOURSELF A PEDICURE

No one has figured out why people's eyes are drawn to feet and shoes, but they are. So, especially in the summer, you might as well have others look at pretty feet. Here's the program:

Soak feet in warm water (or in the bathtub). Scrub with a stiff brush to remove cuticle and dirt.

Massage with hand cream or petroleum jelly. Massage the whole foot, especially around toenails. Push cuticles back gently with a towel.

Clip toenails straight across. Don't curve down into the corners. Don't clip *too* short. Wash away cream.

Stuff pieces of cotton between toes to make polishing easier and to avoid smudging while polish is drying.

Polish toenails all over, bringing polish right up over the ends of the nails. This protects socks and stockings from snags.

HOW TO HAVE BEAUTIFUL HAIR

* *Massage your scalp*—it helps hair grow faster because it stimulates circulation. Massage with fingertips, not fingernails, in a rotating motion.

* *Shampoo your hair at the first sign of oiliness or stringiness.* Don't worry if this is every other day, or even *every* day. As long as you rinse your hair well to remove all traces of soap you won't hurt your hair in the least. (Movie and TV stars have proved this; most of them wash their hair daily.) Do the squeak test: slide thumb and forefinger along a strand of hair. If it squeaks, it's clean. If your fingers glide, keep rinsing.

* *Brush your hair* to clean it, polish it, make it grow. Brush at least 100 strokes a day, using a natural-bristle brush because nylon bristles break hair ends.

* *Shampoo your brush and comb* at the same time you shampoo your hair. Otherwise you'll be putting all the oil or dirt right back into your squeaky-clean hair.

* *Use a conditioner or non-snarl rinse* if you have curly or very dry hair so that you don't tug it all out when combing. BEAUTY FLASH—One of the best and least expensive hair conditioners is crude blackstrap molasses diluted in a cup of warm water and poured over the head. Leave on 1 minute, then rinse—for a real shine. Another trick—just before you leave the shower, turn the cold water on your hair for extra body and sheen.

* *Squeeze out excess moisture* by making a towel-turban.

* *Use a wide-toothed comb* to remove tangles, working up from the ends of the hair toward the scalp.

* *If you have frizzy hair,* you can straighten it with a comb, a brush, and a hair dryer. Start by brushing your hair until there are no snarls left. Then take the comb and separate one section at a time. Hold the section of hair straight out from the scalp. Now take the hair dryer and slide it from the roots down to the ends of the hair you are holding. The hair dryer should be warm, not cold. In effect you're ironing your hair smooth, and it works.

* *If you have baby-fine hair or very dry hair* you can improve its body and shine by massaging a couple of tablespoons of olive or vegetable oil into your scalp about two tours before you plan to shampoo. It does a world of good.

GET RID OF UNWANTED HAIR ON LEGS AND UNDER ARMS

* Wash your legs thoroughly with soap and water—don't

just splash them on. If you shower in the morning, shower first, then shave your legs and underarms. If you could shave in the shower that would be the best place, but it takes skill or you'll hurt yourself.

* Dry hands and, with legs still wet, apply a pre-shave beard softener—yes, the kind your father uses on his beard. It straightens out individual hairs and sets them up for a razor. The emollients in this product are the secret. They have the power to soften and relax tissue.

* Apply shaving lather. Because the legs must be kept moist, it's worth it to buy a good shaving lather because the cheap kind dries too quickly.

* Shave with a good razor, avoiding single-edged blades unless you're very skilled—they make the most cuts. Double-edged blades are good, but heavy. Most fashion models use double-track blades; they're safer.

* Shave with the grain first, then against, to avoid ingrown hairs.

* Forget hot lather devices—they're no more effective than regular.

* Never shave hair on your arms—it will eventually grow back darker and tougher. If you have dark hair on your arms and it worries you, you'll do far better to bleach it with a regular hair bleach from the drugstore.

GET RID OF EYEBROWS THAT ARE TOO BUSHY

But go at it slowly and carefully. If you get carried away, so may one of your only two eyebrows!

* Before tweezing, apply a hot towel to the brows. Using an old toothbrush or an eyebrow brush, brush them up, then sideways. Tweeze them in the direction the hair grows. If the process is painful, go over the area with an ice cube.

* Pluck only one hair at a time. And pull it out in the direction the hair grows.

* Don't pluck hairs above the brow except for a few strays at the end if brows are truly bushy.

* If you use an eyebrow pencil, use one that is just one shade lighter than your hair. Brunettes use dark brown—never black. Brownettes use medium-to-light brown. Redheads use a reddish brown and blondes use an almost gray-silver shade. Apply color with small, light strokes as if you were drawing one hair at a time.

To shape your eyebrows

* Ideally the space between your eyebrows should be the width of your eye, and the brows should begin straight up from the inside corner of your eye. If your eyebrows are too close together, pluck a few hairs to widen the space between them. If they're too skimpy and far apart, pencil in the difference.

* The eyebrow should start full and then taper to a fine hairline at the outer corner of the eye. The outer end should be a teensy bit higher than the beginning point.

~~♨~~

Sitting Pretty

If you're ever on a stage, in a class play, or anyplace where you want to look cool and poised, here are a few pointers about getting into and out of chairs:

1. To approach: pivot around on the balls of your feet until your back is to the chair and you can feel the edge with the calf of your rear leg.

2. Slide rear foot slightly under the chair, and with your back straght, slowly lower yourself into the chair using your knees and thighs, not the upper part of your body.

3. When you rise, reverse the process. With feet close under your body, one in front of the other, push up with the rear foot using your thigh muscles and quickly straighten your legs. This way you're developing beautiful thigh muscles, good posture, and a graceful look. Your body rises *up* in rhythm, instead of plunging forward as though someone had suddenly tipped you out of your chair.

When you sit in a slump you automatically add four inches to the look of your waistline. No one says you have to sit at attention—any more than you have to stand at attention like a soldier—but it's good to know what to do and not to do:

* Try not to seem self-conscious of your arms and legs when you sit down. Compose yourself.

* Keep your knees together one way or another; cross your ankles, placing the left foot behind and to the right of the right foot. Or slide both feet to the right—a jutting-out foot can trip someone passing by.

* You can cross your legs, of course, especially since you wear pants or jeans most of the time. But do it modestly, not like a cowpoke saying, "Wal, whadda ya have to say fer yerself?" If you are overweight, forget it—crossing your legs emphasizes their size. Also, if you're on a stage or platform and are wearing a dress, don't take the chance.

* If you're nervous, here's a trick: put both hands, palms up, in your lap and place the thumb of one hand in the palm of the other. It looks natural and relaxed. Besides, it gives you something to hold.

Don'ts for sitting

* Don't fuss, arranging your skirt after you are seated. It's prissy.

* Don't let your underclothes show.

* Don't let your feet be pigeon-toed.

* Don't let your knees separate.

Learn to Walk
the Way
Fashion Models Do

Even if your figure is perfect, a sloppy or heavy-footed walk can spoil the whole impression you make. And strangely enough, if your figure still has a long way to go a graceful walk will make up for it. Boys and men instinctively turn to watch the way a woman walks, and a beauty queen is judged as much by her walk as her figure. One of the first things a model must learn is how to walk, turn, and pivot. Here are the things you can practice in your own bedroom with or without a book on your head (the book helps you to hold yourself high) and with or without music (music helps set a rhythm):

1. Find some area in your house where you can take five steps—that's all, just five. Put a string, chalk mark, or tape on the floor to indicate a straight line. If you can practice in front of a full-length mirror all the better; you'll see yourself as others see you.

2. Get off your heels, get your chin level, back straight, pelvis under, chest up, tummy in, and walk with the

grace of a native woman carrying a basket on her head and wearing no shoes. This will help you when you try your first pair of heels. There's nothing more awkward than a girl who *shows* it's her first time in higher heels!

3. Take steps no longer than the length of your own foot.
4. Your toes should point straight ahead or be turned slightly outward, as models and dancers walk.
5. There should be no noticeable change of weight from one foot to the other. To achieve this, keep the weight on the balls of your feet and "push off" with the ball of the back foot.
6. Keep knees flexed so they act as springs.
7. Put one foot directly in front of the other on one line.
8. Move your arms in opposition to your feet—when the right foot is forward, the left arm swings forward, and vice versa.
9. Swing arms from shoulders with your elbows held close to your body but not tight. Keep your arms relaxed and don't bend your elbows as your arms come forward.
10. "Float" from the waistline up, walk from the waistline down, and control your walk from your midriff.

To pivot

A pivot is simply a graceful, balanced turn. Take five steps, ending with your left foot in front. Turn to the right by coming onto the balls of both feet and pivoting your body toward the right until you are facing in your original position. As you turn, stop your left foot as soon as it is at a 45-degree angle to the line, but let the right foot continue to pivot until its entire length is on the line. Then draw the right foot back toward the instep of the left. Voila!

Stairs can lead to heavenly-shaped thighs

You climb so *many* stairs, especially at school, that you might as well learn how you can turn this day-in, day-out effort into a system to improve the shape of your legs, whether they're a bit too chubby or too skinny. Here's how:

* Keep your knees flexed at all times—don't bend and straighten them as you climb stairs. Let the large muscles in your thighs do the work and watch how your upper legs become trimmer and slimmer.

* Keep your body upright when you walk up steps.

* Place your entire foot on each step. If stairs are too narrow, turn both feet in one direction going up or down stairs.

* Look with your eyes, not your head. You'll never see

fashion models bending their heads down to look at steps (of course, it takes practice).

* When coming down steps, your weight should go into toes first, then heel; otherwise you thump. And don't turn your knees outward as if you were carrying a heavy bundle.

How to Care For, Cut, and Style the Hair You Were Born With

Baby-fine hair

SHAMPOO with protein shampoo to add body.
CUT with a blunt cut, not LAYERED, for more body.
STYLE in smooth, straight lines.
RINSE with protein rinse for more bounce.
DON'T overbrush fine hair.

Bushy and curly hair

SHAMPOO with a creme or oil shampoo.
CUT wet and follow natural waves.
STYLE short if you don't want to set it. If you want your hair to *grow* long, set it in large rollers for a smooth look.
RINSE with a creme rinse; use heated oil treatments monthly.
DON'T attempt to straighten your hair at home unless an adult helps you.

Coarse and wiry hair

SHAMPOO with a creme or oil shampoo.
CUT your hair when wet, and never shorter than 5 to 6 inches from crown.
STYLE in a close-to-the-head look; easier if you keep your hair medium length.
RINSE with a creme rinse.
DON'T cut your hair too short; don't use a blunt cut; don't try home permanents unless an adult helps you.

Thick and straight hair

SHAMPOO with a creme shampoo.
CUT your hair while wet and taper the ends.
STYLE as you like—the sky's the limit; yours is the kind of hair everyone dreams of.
RINSE with a creme rinse; use oil treatments monthly.
DON'T cut your hair blunt; it will look like a wig.

Naturally wavy hair

SHAMPOO with castile or plain shampoo if hair is normal; use special shampoo for dandruff or oily hair.
CUT to follow natural waves; hard to do yourself, so go to a hairdresser.
STYLE short or medium for best look.
RINSE with vinegar or lemon rinse.
DON'T cut hair dry; don't try to straighten at home unless someone helps you.

Your Voice – How Many Decibels?

Unless you come from a family of actors or entertainers, the odds are that no one has given you an honest opinion about the *sound* of your voice. Parents and teachers say, "Not so loud over there!" or "Quiet, qui-i-i-ettt!" but that isn't exactly voice training, which you'll get in a high school public speaking course later on.

The best way to find out how you sound is to talk into a tape recorder, then listen for flaws you want to correct:

* A harsh or loud voice sounds bossy.

* A monotone voice is boring.

* Talking too fast tires people just listening to you.

* Slurring, dropping ends of words (talkin', walkin', doin', nothin'), or mispronouncing key words you use every day ("fer" for "for," "ta" for "to," "ya" for "you") make you sound like a country bumpkin. Also avoid didja, what-cha, whyja, and howja.

* Poor grammar is childish; avoid such baby habits as "me and Nancy went to the library."

If you don't have a tape recorder, listen to your voice either of these two ways:

1. Say something with your nose almost against the center of a large half-opened magazine. You will hear your voice magnified.
2. Face a corner of a room, standing as close as you can to where the walls meet. Cup your hands slightly over your ears and speak in your usual voice. The sound will bounce back amplified and you may be surprised at what you hear.

PRIVATE TIP—You can have the most sexy voice in town, but if you have bad breath no one will stand near enough to hear you. Bad breath comes from an upset stomach, or from garlic, onions, and other smelly foods. However, one of the biggest causes is poor tooth brushing after meals. If you brush your teeth before coming to breakfast, fine, but then brush again after you eat, and use a mouthwash. Just plain baking soda in cool water is an easy one. Ditto after lunch if you possibly can. If you eat lunch at school, use a breath spray when you've brought a salami sandwich.

What to talk about if you're shy or nervous

It's a breeze to talk all night long with your close girlfriends, but a different story when it comes to talking to adults. Just remember that adults are interested in what interests *you*. They really hate asking the same tired old "What grade are you in now?" but unless you volunteer a few sentences, they're stuck without a clue to your real self. For lack of any earth-shaking information, the best topic is the most recent one—whatever you have just been doing, reading, working at within the last few hours. It will still be fresh to you and to any adult listening.

Talking to a boy is sometimes harder

1. Stop worrying about how you look. Ask a boy questions—not personal prying ones, but his opinions about sports, TV, hobbies, the car he'd like to own, music, pets, and books.

2. When conversation lags, have a few topics up your sleeve—his horoscope sign and what that means. Try a compliment, but be sincere. Admire his shirt or tie or bicycle, compliment him on his dancing or the last game you watched him play—but don't gush and don't try to pump compliments from him. If he says something flattering, say, "Thank you," and smile; don't say, "You must be crazy; this is an old rag." That's a put-down.

3. Avoid tedious details when you tell a story. Get to the point and leave out all the little useless facts.

4. When you don't know anything about a subject, ask questions. Boys love to turn instructor now and then.

5. When all else fails, you can always sigh and say, "Do you have as hard a time as I do talking to people?" It's often the case.

A Few
Telephone Manners

* *When you telephone a friend,* say hello first, then your name: "Hello, this is Sally Smith." Then ask for the person you're calling: "May I speak to Geraldine, please?" Even if your friend or her parents recognize your voice you should always say who you are.

* *If the person you called is not there* don't just say, "OK," and hang up. Say you'll call back, or ask her to please call you. Then say, "Thank you" and "Goodbye."

* *When you answer the phone* and it's for someone else, say, "Just a moment, please," then put the phone down and find the person being called to tell her she's wanted on the phone. Don't scream from where you're standing—it could momentarily deafen the caller, or at least scare the wits out of him.

* *When the call is for someone who isn't home,* say, "He isn't home (or here); would you like to leave a message?" Then make a note of the message instead of trusting to divine guidance that you'll remember it.

* *When you answer the phone in your own home,* just say, "Hello," not "Brown residence!"—you'll sound like a butler or a secretary.

AN AGE-OLD RULE—The person who phones is the one who should end the conversation and say goodbye. Not the main issue at your present age, perhaps, but nice to know for the future.

New People: Meeting, Greeting, and Introducing Others

You can get by with a simple, hurried "Hi!" in most school yards, movie theater lobbies, and public places, but the crunch comes when you want to introduce someone important in just the right way. Or if you want to make a good impression when you are being introduced to new people, young or old.

Here are the basic rules of the introduction game. It's easy—and absolutely necessary—to memorize them.

WHAT A BOY DOES WHEN HE IS BEING INTRODUCED

1. *He stands up* when he is introduced to women, girls, men, and even other boys—there are no exceptions. And no excuse for remaining seated unless his leg is in a cast.
2. *He shakes hands* with men and boys, but he hesitates before offering his hand to be shaken by women and girls. He watches; if the woman or girl holds out her hand he shakes it, of course.

In many parts of the world hand-shaking customs are different. In France, for instance, young boys and girls begin shaking hands with each other as soon as they learn how. Girls shake hands with girls and women with women, and not just when they're meeting for the first time either—they shake hands whenever they greet their friends. In Mexico, if you don't offer to shake hands you insult the person you're meeting, so Mexican tourism booklets warn visitors about this potential hazard as seriously as they warn against drinking the local tap water.

3. *He says, "How do you do?"* to anyone in the older generation (21 years old and up). Also, when meeting older men, he adds "sir." For instance, to a friend's father he would say, "How do you do, sir?" To friends his own age he can say anything from "Hello" to "Hey, man," "Hi there," or "Howdy," just as long as he stands up and gets the handshake going while saying it.

4. *He practices until he develops a good manly handshake.* It takes only a few minutes of trials and errors with his own family, both male and female members, to hit the right pressure between wet washcloth and temporary crippler. It's sad, but only someone who truly cares will ever tell a boy he has a weak or clammy handshake. And it's also unfortunate that a limp, open-palm handshake means a questionable character reference to some people. On the plus side, a boy is often noticed or complimented for his manly, spontaneous handshake even before he's done anything else memorable.

5. *He looks at the person to whom he is being introduced.* He doesn't have to stare deeply into the other's eyes—a glance with a nod or smile will do. The trick is to avoid looking down (shyness) or into space (lost and at sea).

WHAT A GIRL DOES WHEN SHE
IS BEING INTRODUCED

1. *She stands up* whenever she is being introduced to an adult, male or female. Later on, when she is over 21 herself, she may stay seated when introduced to the average man or woman, shaking hands or simply nodding an acknowledgment of the introduction without standing up. There are exceptions, however:

   * *When men or women are much, much older* so that their age itself demands respect (a friend's grandmother).

   * *When people are VIPs (Very Important Persons)* to be honored for their achievements, special roles in life (a school principal, a priest, or a nun), or titles (the mayor, the wife of a congressman). In such cases, a girl stands up whether it's a man or woman she's meeting.

2. *She offers to shake hands* with all older people, male or female, until she's an adult herself. With her own age group, she can decide whether she wants to be a handshaker or a smile-and-nodder. Shaking hands is first choice for two reasons: It's a natural ice-breaker because it puts boys at ease immediately; and secondly, it gives a girl something definite to do during the few crucial seconds it takes to meet someone new, girl or boy.

3. *She says, "How do you do?"* to all adults. To people her own age she can say "Hi," "Hello," or "How are you?" even though she'll rarely find out. She may add, "I'm so glad (happy) to meet you," if she really means it.

4. *She sits down first* if she has been introduced in a room where there are men or boys who won't sit down while a girl or woman is still standing up.

MAKING INTRODUCTIONS

From one generation to another and finally down to yours, certain rules of order have been formulated for introducing people to each other. To master them, visualize four totem poles, each with a top figure that is more important than the one below.

The first totem pole denotes different age groups.

An older person's name tops a younger person's name (even if the older person is a male).

The second totem pole denotes females and males.

A woman's name tops a man's name.

The third totem pole shows girl-friends and boyfriends your own age.

A girl's name tops a boy's name.

The fourth totem pole stands for family relationships.

An adult's name tops a child's name.

You start an introduction by saying the top (more important) name first, followed by any of these phrases:

"(Mrs. Smith), this is . . ."
"(Mrs. Smith), have you met . . . ?"
"(Mrs. Smith), may I present . . . ?" (more formal)

You must look at each person as you say his or her name. There's a reason: If you don't actually turn toward the person you're introducing, you'll fall into the old hitch-hiker's thumb game, pointing at your friend as if he were someone you hailed along the roadside.

Here's how it all works out.

INTRODUCING PEOPLE OF DIFFERENT AGES: Say the older person's name first because a younger person is always presented TO an older one:

"Mr. Jones, . . . this is . . . my brother Joe."

INTRODUCING ADULT WOMEN AND MEN: Say the woman's name first because a man is always presented TO a woman:

"Miss Jones, . . . this is . . . Dr. Smith."

INTRODUCING GIRLFRIENDS AND BOYFRIENDS IN YOUR OWN AGE GROUP: Say the girl's name first because a boy is always presented TO a girl:

"Sally, . . . this is . . . Joe Smith."

Since you've used Sally's first name only, you complete the introduction by turning toward Sally and filling in her last name: "Sally Jones."

INTRODUCING MEMBERS OF YOUR FAMILY: Say the adult's name first because a child or younger person is always presented TO an adult:

"Dad, . . . this is . . . Roger Smith."

Here's how to conduct special introductions

INTRODUCING A FAMILY MEMBER WHOSE LAST NAME IS DIFFER-
ENT FROM YOURS: This could be a maternal grandparent, an
aunt, uncle, or cousin; or your mother if she has remarried.
You say, "Mrs. Smith, this is my grandmother, Mrs.
French." Or, in a case where you mother's married name is
now different: "This is Mr. Jones"; then looking again at
your mother, you add, "My mother, Mrs. Brown."

INTRODUCING ONE PERSON TO A GROUP OF PEOPLE: To a group
of ten people or less, you should first present the newcomer
informally to the group at large: ("Hey, everybody, this is
Sally Smith.") then follow through by introducing the new
person to each member of the group as you move from one
to another.

To a larger group, your best bet is to introduce the
newcomer to the first two or three people nearby, with the
fond hope that they will carry on further introductions to
other group members. You don't stop the clock—and the
fun—while you lead the newcomer from one person to another, ending with, "Did I skip anyone?" There's usually no
answer, and no easy way to revive the mood you've abruptly
altered.

INTRODUCTIONS TO DIGNITARIES

From here to the Far East, countries have so many different
titles for their leaders that even our President has a chief of
protocol to deal with the rules and customs of diplomats,
the military, and members of courts. So don't worry about
how you should address a duke's son or a French cabinet

minister. Every etiquette book has a thick chapter devoted solely to forms of address, spoken and written, for foreign and domestic dignitaries. When you're actually sure you're going to visit the state or national capital—where you might be introduced to a VIP—or a foreign country, you can always do a crash course on fine points.

However, in your own world today, there ARE certain people you should know how to address since they are not called Mr., Mrs., or Miss. It's embarrassing to goof and find yourself saying "Mister Smith" loud and clear just as you overhear the man addressed as *Doctor* (or Admiral or Senator!) Smith.

Here are some of the forms you're likely to need in the near future.

TO MEMBERS OF THE CLERGY	YOU SAY
A Priest	"Father Smith"
A Catholic Nun	"Sister Annunciata" or "Sister"
A Rabbi	"Rabbi Saks" or "Rabbi"
A Cantor	"Cantor Love"
A Protestant Minister	"Sir" or "Doctor Jones" (The terms "Reverend" or "The Reverend John Jones" are used only when you are introducing or referring to a minister, not when you are simply saying "How do you do?" to him.)
An Archdeacon	"Mr. Archdeacon"
A Dean	"Mr. Dean" or "Dean Brown"
A Protestant Bishop	"Bishop Jones"
A Catholic Bishop	"Your Grace"
A Catholic Archbishop	"Your Excellency"

| A Catholic Cardinal | "Your Eminence" |
| The Pope | "Your Holiness" |

TO GOVERNMENT OFFICIALS	YOU SAY
A Mayor	"Mayor Smith" or "Mr. Mayor"
A Governor	"Governor Jones"
A Congressman (U.S. or State)	"Mr. Smith"
A Senator (U.S. or State)	"Senator Jones"
A Foreign Ambassador	"Mr. Ambassador"
An American Ambassador	"Mr. Ambassador" or "Mr. Bruce"
A Supreme Court Justice	"Mr. Justice"
The Chief Justice	"Mr. Chief Justice" (When introducing or referring to the Chief Justice of the Supreme Court, you say, *The* Chief Justice.")
A Cabinet Officer	"Mr. Secretary"
The Vice-President of the U.S.	"Mr. Vice-President"
The President of the U.S.	"Mr. President" (In lengthy conversations, "Sir" may be used occasionally.)

TO MEMBERS OF THE MILITARY IN THE ARMY, AIR FORCE AND MARINE CORPS	YOU SAY
Any General (Brigadier or 5-Star)	"General Jones"
A Colonel or Lt. Colonel	"Colonel Jones"
A Lieutenant or	"Lieutenant Jones"

First Lieutenant	
A Major or a Captain	"Major Jones,"
	"Captain Jones"
A Cadet	"Mr. Smith"
A Corporal	"Corporal Jones"
A Warrant Officer	"Mister Jones"

IN THE NAVY	YOU SAY
AND COAST GUARD	
An Admiral (including Fleet, Vice, or Rear)	"Admiral Jones"
A Commodore	"Commodore Jones"
A Captain (or any officer in command of a ship regardless of his usual title)	"Captain Jones"
A Commander or Lt. Commander	"Commander Jones"
Midshipman, Ensign, Warrant Officer, Lieutenant or Lieutenant, Junior Grade	"Mr. Jones"
A Military Chaplain	"Chaplain" or "Chaplain Jones" (regardless of his actual rank)
A Military Doctor	"Doctor Jones" until he reaches Captain or above; then you specify his rank: "Major," "Colonel," or "General Jones"

GIRLS AND WOMEN SHAKE HANDS TOO

Unless you want to go on curtsying until you're in high school, it's good to shake hands—it gives you something to do when you're meeting people for the first time. It's a warm, friendly gesture toward boys as well as girls. A boy or a man will wait for you to extend your hand first. However, you should hesitate before flinging out your hand when you are introduced to an older woman. If she doesn't offer hers, you keep yours at your side and just nod when you're introduced.

The main thing to avoid is a "wet dishrag" handshake that is so limp the other person might think you were going to faint, or a straight-out hand instead of a nice, friendly grasp. When you're introduced, look at the other person's eyes, say, "How do you do," and literally take hold of the other person's hand, shaking it firmly and briefly.

DOORWAY MANNERS

When the doorbell rings and your parents are home, it's best to ask if they want you to answer the door. If they say yes, don't rush to swing open the door as if you expected a delegation from another planet. Just quietly open the door, say "Hello," and—*if it's a friend*—invite her or him in. Then say you'll tell your mother (sister, brother, father, whoever) the friend is here. Show the friend into the living room while you find the person involved.

Unless your mother can appear immediately, return to the living room and talk to—or at least sit with—the friend until your mother appears. If you've just made a batch of cookies, it's fine to say, "I just made some sugar cookies; would you like one?" but you don't have to feed a visitor the moment she or he enters your house.

If it's a stranger, open the door, say, "Hello," and either listen to his request or ask, "What is it?" Do not invite a stranger into your house. Say, "Please wait here and I'll call my mother." Then close the door and tell an adult in your family what the stranger wants.

Basic Table Manners for Almost Any Occasion

Odds are your mother has a job, and just to keep your body and soul together, you've made do with quick, easy meals at the kitchen counter, snack bars, carry-outs, maybe even standing up and "eating from the pan to save washing the plate." No wonder you get the shakes just thinking about setting a dinner table or sitting around one at a party. Relax. You'll behave like a pro as soon as you've practiced setting a table by yourself a few times. Try it for two people, then four, and eventually work up to six. Even if you work with paper napkins, plastic glasses, and kitchen silver, the rules will be the same wherever you go.

A BASIC PLACE SETTING

1. Butter spreader
2. Bread and butter plate
3. Meat fork
4. Salad fork
5. Dinner plate
6. Soup plate
7. Salad knife
8. Meat knife
9. Oval soup spoon
10. Seafood cocktail fork
    (It may also be placed at
    an angle so prongs rest in
    bowl of soup spoon.)
11. Water goblet
12. Wine glass

THE INFORMAL SETTING
YOU WILL USE MOST OFTEN

TIPS TO MEMORIZE AND REMEMBER

Silver

All silver (except for the dessert course) is placed in the order it is used. If you are going to serve soup, place the soup cups and their saucers on top of the service plate, with soup spoons at the far right. If your first course will be salad, put the salad forks to the left of the regular forks and, of course, eliminate the soup spoons.

Napkins

A dinner napkin is folded flat and can be placed neatly either on each place plate or to the left of the plate. If you are going to put food on the plates before guests sit down, place the napkin to the left of the plate on the far side of the silver.

A luncheon napkin is smaller and should be folded like a man's pocket handkerchief with corners pointing down toward the edge of the table. The top corner is then folded under and creased to stay folded. If you are going to have a first course on the plate when guests sit down, put the napkin to the left of the plate.

When a hostess picks up her napkin, unfold yours (without shaking it like an amateur magician), keeping it folded in half if it's a large dinner napkin, with the open edges toward you. If it's a smaller luncheon napkin, unfold it all the way.

When you're in a restaurant, pick up, unfold, and place your napkin on your lap as soon as everyone is seated.

Sometimes novelty napkin rings are used to pep up a table. If so, slide it off the napkin and place it to the left of your plate or above your plate.

Use napkins for a light dab, not for towels. Blot your lips before you sip from a glass to remove any oil or food particles which might stick to the rim of the glass.

When you leave the table—having been excused by the host or hostess either during the course of the dinner or at the end—lay your napkin to the left of your plate, slightly folded over. Don't place it on your empty chair. Don't fold a used napkin or put it back into a napkin ring unless you're at home and you're expected to use the same one again.

Glasses

Glasses are placed above and to the right of the dinner plate. If more than one size is used, the smaller one goes in front of the larger one so it won't be hidden. Therefore, a wine glass is in front of a water goblet. When you drink wine, pick up the glass by the stem, not the bowl of the glass. The "bowl bit" is a way of "warming" fine old brandy; you've seen it done in English movies, but that's a long way off for you!

Before you begin to eat

* *Boys and men let girls and women walk ahead of them* into the dining room and to the table. Guests stand behind their chairs until the hostess sits down. Boys and men hold chairs for girls and women. Here's the way it's done: The boy stands behind the girl's chair and, with both hands on the upper part of the chair, pulls it out slowly. The girl slips into the chair by moving to her right. The boy then gently pushes the chair under her and in toward the table.

* *When there are place cards* they may sometimes be on top of your napkin in the middle of the plate. In that case, just pick yours up and put it on the table above your plate before you unfold your napkin.

* *If grace is said* you will be given some advance notice by the hostess. One clue: if she sits quietly before picking up her napkin, you can be pretty sure a grace will be said. In that case, leave your napkin in place, too, until after the blessing is over.

* *Sometimes the host serves from a stack of plates* in front of him or on a cart beside him. There is a certain ritual you should know about: The host passes the first filled plate to

the girl or woman on his right. She gives him her empty plate in exchange. He uses that empty plate to fill and serve the first woman on his left, continuing the pattern of "right" and then "left" until all women are served. The hostess is not served first, but is the last woman to be served. Then the host serves the men at the table, and himself last.

* *Food may be passed at a casual dinner,* but remember to PASS—DON'T SLIDE—dishes from yourself to another guest. Set a bowl or serving dish down at your left (unless you are left-handed) and pass to the right.

* *When a meal is served by a maid* or a household helper, food is presented to you at your left, mostly because more people are right-handed than left-handed. Pick up the serving spoon with your right hand, the fork with your left. Use the spoon to lift a portion of meat or vegetable onto your plate, holding the fork lightly on top of the portion you're transferring so that it won't slip off the spoon. After you have served yourself, place the serving fork and spoon side by side on the platter or in the dish. Food is served first to the woman or girl sitting at the right of the host (or hostess if no host is there). Then service continues around the table.

During the dinner

* *You may start eating* at a large dinner after several persons have been served, mainly to avoid letting good food get cold. Of course, at a small dinner it's better to wait until everyone has been served and the hostess has begun eating.

* *Seconds* are not only permitted, they're encouraged. Most

79

hostesses are overjoyed when people ask for or accept seconds. Just be sure when you pass your plate that your knife and fork are well balanced on the plate—not on the edge—so they won't fall off.

* *Before you leave the table at the end of dinner,* wait for the hostess to signal that she's going to get up. She does this by placing her napkin at the left of her plate, then rising.

* *A finger bowl* is a rarity except in homes with lots of servants and formality. However, you may be served a finger bowl on the dessert plate just before dessert is served. There will be a doily under the bowl and dessert silver alongside. Here is what you do. First, pick up the dessert fork and lay it at the left of the dessert plate, then place the spoon at the right. Pick up the finger bowl, doily and all, and put it on the table above your dessert fork. After dessert, dip the tips of your fingers—one hand at a time—into the water in the finger bowl and dry them on the napkin in your lap. If your mouth feels sticky, moisten your fingertips and dab your lips, then dry them quickly with your napkin.

Seat boy, girl, boy, girl as much as possible. The male guest of honor sits at the hostess's right; the female guest of honor at the host's right. All girls? If there's a guest of honor, she is seated at the hostess's right. All boys? Ditto. The guest of honor is on the host's right.

THE THREE WORST EATING HABITS

1. Chewing food with your lips open while emitting a smacking sound even a mother can't love. It's not enough to know your *teeth are together* chewing in happy unison; your lips must be closed—not clamped together but definitely together and touching. That way no slurpy, slapping sounds will escape.
2. Cutting all the meat on your plate at once. It's not only wrong, and a tiring chore, but it leaves your plate looking like a dog's dish. Cut one piece of meat at a time and eat it.
3. Cutting one's meat cello-playing style. Some 69.78

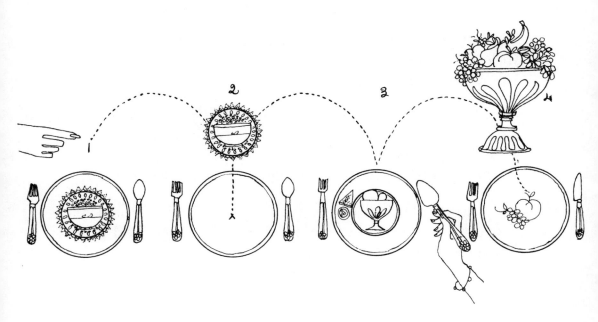

percent of all males, young and old, do it. Some girls do, too. Perhaps it's more fun stabbing an innocent lamb chop in the back with a straight-up fork, then sawing it to death with a cruel knife. But it still isn't nice to watch. Hold your fork at an angle, low to the plate, and the same with your knife. The idea is to be cool and competent.

SOME FOODS ARE DIFFICULT TO EAT— BUT WORTH IT

Vegetables

CORN ON THE COB. Should be buttered and seasoned a small area at a time, then held firmly and eaten one bite at a time. Butter for corn should be placed on the bread-and-butter plate and used as needed.

BAKED POTATOES. If the potato isn't slit open, use your knife to cut an opening and then break it open further with your fork. Use your fork to mix butter and seasonings with the potato. (Always use a fork instead of a knife to mix butter with vegetables on your plate.)

FRENCH-FRIED POTATOES. Use your fork to break off each bite unless you are at a picnic or barbecue; then you can eat them with your fingers.

ASPARAGUS. Use your fork to cut off and eat one bite at a time. Leave the tough ends on your plate. Don't try to tilt your head back and eat fresh asparagus like a sword swallower—you'll just have to change your shirt after dinner.

ARTICHOKES. Served hot or cold, you pull off one leaf at a time, dip the base of the leaf in butter or sauce, and pull it between your teeth to "scrape off" the edible part. Discard

the rest of the leaf and put it on the side of the plate before going on to the next leaf. When you reach the cone-shaped heart of the artichoke, hold it with your fork and cut off the fuzzy "choke" with your knife, set it aside because it is inedible, and eat the heart with your fork, first dipping each bite in the sauce.

Meat, fish, seafood, poultry

SHRIMP. Small ones served as a cocktail are éaten whole with your cocktail fork. Larger ones may be cut if they're served on a plate. If they're in a cocktail dish, it's perfectly OK to spear a shrimp with your fork and bite off half as you hold it on the fork.

A WHOLE FISH. If the head is on (rare), cut it off first. Then slit the fish from head to tail with your knife as you steady it with your fork. Open the fish out flat, using your knife and fork, and insert the tip of the knife under the backbone.

Gently lift it out whole. While eating, remove any small fish bones from your mouth with your thumb and forefinger and place them on your plate. In most restaurants, waiters prepare fish for you; if they haven't done so, ask them to.

LOBSTER. First break off small claws with your fingers and quietly suck or chew out the meat. Use a shell-cracker to break open the large claws. Pull them apart with your fingers and remove the meat with a fish fork. The large pieces of lobster from the body and tail are eaten with your fork. Because lobsters are often messy to eat, restaurants furnish bibs, oversized napkins, and finger bowls of warm water and lemon juice to get you back in shape.

CLAMS. When eating clams on the half-shell, pry the clam out with your oyster fork while holding the shell with the other hand. When clams are steamed, the shell usually opens up and you can use your fingers to pry them farther apart. Don't use your knife for this. Lift out the clam with your fork, dip it in melted butter or sauce, and eat it whole. Place empty shells on your bread-and-butter plate if a special bowl isn't provided.

CHICKEN. Overcivilized as it mayseem, even fried chicken pieces should be eaten with a knife and fork unless you're outdoors at a picnic or you're eating at a drive-in. Use your knife to cut the meat from the bone while you hold it with your fork.

Fruit

HALF GRAPEFRUIT. If the fruit hasn't been cut into sections, dig into each section slowly so that the juice will not squirt. Scoop up juice by spoonfuls—don't pick up the grapefruit and squeeze the juice into your spoon unless you're all alone in the kitchen and want to rebel.

FRESH APRICOTS, PLUMS, PEACHES. Hold in your fingers and bite the fruit off the pit. If you accidentally get the pit in your mouth, remove it with your fingers. Some peaches have freestones; they can be cut in half and the pit removed.

APPLES AND PEARS. Cut the fruit in quarters, core, and peel. Then eat with your fingers or with a fruit knife and fork.

BANANAS. Only on a picnic should a partially peeled banana be brought to the mouth with its peeling hanging down while you chomp it down. Much better to completely remove the skin, put it on the side of your plate, then break off pieces of the banana and eat them with your fingers.

ORANGES AND TANGERINES. Slit the thick rind in several places with a knife, from top to bottom. Remove the rind with your fingers, then pull the fruit sections apart and eat one at a time.

FRUIT COCKTAIL. Eat with a spoon.

STEWED FRUIT. Eat with a spoon.

FRUIT SALAD. Use a fork, even if it's served with a scoop of sherbet.

GRAPES. Pull or cut off a small bunch from the large bunch. Eat one grape at a time, putting the whole grape in your mouth. Take seeds from your mouth one at a time after you have chewed and swallowed the fruit.

BERRIES. Use a spoon to eat raspberries, blueberries, any small berries. When whole fresh strawberries are served with a sugar dip, pick up the strawberry by the stem, dip it into the sugar, and bite the whole berry from the stem. If the strawberry is a prize-winner, bite off half, without dripping the juice.

AVOCADOS. When filled with salad, use your fork. When served in the shell with salad dressing only, use a spoon.

MELON. When cut in little cubes or balls as a cocktail, use a spoon. Eat watermelon with a fork. Most of the seeds can be easily pushed aside with the fork. If some get in your mouth, remove them by hand, after you have swallowed the fruit, and put the seeds on your plate.

Miscellaneous

BREAD AND ROLLS. Break off a small portion, butter it over your plate, and finish eating the piece before you break off another. Don't hold bread flat in the palm of your hand while you spread butter on it.

SPAGHETTI AND SAUCE. The easiest way is the Italian way: In your left hand hold a large spoon tilted down toward the plate, the edge touching the plate. Using the fork in your

right hand, wind the spaghetti as you twist the fork against the spoon. Then quickly bring the morsel to your mouth before it slithers off the fork.

SHISH KEBAB. Hold the meat-filled spear in one hand, your fork in the other against the handle of the spear. As you pull the spear, push the food off with your fork onto your plate, then eat each piece with your fork.

SOUP. Whether soup is served in a soup or bouillon cup, or in a large soup plate, work the spoon away from you. Don't overfill the spoon. Carry it to the mouth quietly; avoid slurping sounds. The cup or plate may be tilted away from you to dip up last spoonfuls. Leave spoon on the saucer *beside* a soup cup—or *in* a soup plate. Clear bouillon or broth may be drunk if it's in a cup with one or two handles. Never blow on soup to cool it.

GRAVY. Ladle gravy from the gravy boat—don't pour it. If you like bread soaked in gravy, first put a small piece of bread on the gravy in your plate and eat it with a knife and fork as you would eat meat.

PETITS FOURS (miniature dessert cakes and small cookies). Eat with your fingers.

CANDY IN PAPER FRILLS. Pick up both frill and candy from the plate (without pinching to see what flavors there are to choose from) and take the candy out of the frill to eat.

TEA WITH TEA BAG. Remove tea bag with your teaspoon, pressing it lightly against inside of cup to prevent filling your saucer with tea, and place bag on saucer beside cup.

Going Shopping

Shopping is an important and fun part of your life, especially now when malls and marts are part of every city or suburb. Whether you're driven to a store by your parent or go alone on your bike, once inside there are helpful things to know:

* Wait for your turn without trying to push ahead of other customers and without shouting questions over their heads to the salesperson.

* Take care of merchandise you're trying on, even if you don't like it or intend to buy it. Put things back on hangers or across the back of a chair. Make sure you receive a sales slip when you buy something in case you have to return it later.

* Make returns within the time limit specified on the sales slip (yes, it's there, in the fine print). You know that swim suits and underwear can never be returned so try them on carefully before you pay for them.

* If a salesperson is slow or old, be patient. Deep sighs from your weary soul won't speed up a thing.

* If a salesperson is rude to you because you're young, be civil and firm. Say, "My mother will be here soon but she asked me to start looking at swim suits." If you make good sense, perhaps the snooty salesperson will climb down from her high horse and consider you a customer—which you are!

* If you have a complaint about soiled or ripped merchandise, and your mother is somewhere in the store, wait for her to go to the desk and ask for the department manager. If you have to go through this alone, stick to the facts and avoid throwing out a few choice insults—you'll get nowhere that way.

* It's fun to help a friend—or have a friend help you—select clothes, but it's childish when the whole club tries to crowd into the fitting room and voice-vote each other down on what you should buy.

BUYING YOUR FIRST BRA

Before you shop for a pre-teen bra, measure yourself. Keep the tape measure flat and snug, measuring directly under your bust. Then add five inches to determine the size you need. Example: an under-bust measurement of 29 inches means a size 34 bra. If you are an in-between size, order the next largest size.

In the store, go to the pre-teen or teen lingerie department. Because it's your first time, say, "May I try these on alone?" Both your mother and the salesperson will understand.

In the fitting room

Slide straps over the shoulders, then lean forward from the waist to fit your breasts into the cups. Straighten up, fasten the bra, and adjust it. Run a finger under the band across the back to smooth it. There are four cup sizes: AA (Extra Small), A (Small), B (Average), and C (Full bust).

How to tell if it fits right

* When seated, can you move comfortably; take a good deep breath?

* Are the breasts crowded together? If so, the cup size is too small.

* Can you run your finger easily under the band of the bra? If not, the bra is too tight.

* Do the breasts fill out the cup? If not, a smaller cup may be needed, or detachable pads.

* Do bulges appear under your arms? If so, a larger size is needed.

Going to Restaurants

It's a treat to get away from quick snacks at the kitchen counter, hurried school lunches, and carry-out food, and be taken to a real restaurant where you're treated like a princess and you have all those choices on the menu! The first two or three times your parents will tell you what to do, but for the future it's nice to know some of the things that happen in any restaurant from the ones in your town to the Eiffel Tower restaurant in Paris.

* Check rooms are for boys' and men's hats and coats. A girl wears her coat to the table, sits down, and removes it after she is seated by just dropping the top part over the back of the chair. Of course, if your raincoat and umbrella are soaked, you check them at the same time the boy checks his coat.

* If there is a headwaiter, host, or hostess to seat people, girls and women follow directly behind him or her, with boys and men bringing up the rear. If there is no head-

waiter or similar functionary, the boy or man goes ahead to find a table, and the girl follows him.

* *Table seatings* go this way: at open tables, women and girls sit across from each other; at wall tables, sometimes called banquettes (pronounced bonk-etz), women sit in the wall seats, boys on the chairs opposite.

HOW TO ORDER

* After you sit down, pick up your napkin FIRST and put it in your lap, and then drink some water, butter some bread if it's already on the table, eat a pickle, look at the menu, whatever. Boys and men order for women; however, a girl talks directly to the waiter when he asks about salad dressing, choice of a sauce or side dish, or how she wants her steak done.

* "Table d'hôte" means one price for the whole dinner. "A la carte" means a separate price for each item ordered, so a la carte translates to "expensive."

* You address a waiter as "Waiter," not "boy." You never clap your hands or snap your fingers to get a waiter's or waitress's attention. If your raised hand or slightly raised voice doesn't bring the waiter over, you stop another one and ask him to please send your waiter to your table.

* Once you've decided what you want from the menu, don't keep changing your order—it makes you seem wishy-washy.

* If you have a complaint—the silver or glass isn't clean, the food tastes suspicious or badly cooked—let your parents or the boy call the waiter over to complain in a reasonable

voice. Don't wipe your silver with your napkin, tap your glass in indignation, or throw your hands up in disgust.

* If you're eating in a restaurant where a buffet table is the main attraction, you may go back more than once. However, you first sit down at the table, remove your coat, put your handbag on the table (or under it, if the bag is bulky), and then go to the buffet table. When you go back for seconds, leave your used dishes and silver in place and a bus boy will remove them while you're at the buffet table. Take a clean plate for your next course.

* When friends stop by your table in a restaurant, boys and men stand up to greet girls and women, and they remain standing until the friends go on to their own table. Girls and women stay seated as they are introduced to the passers-by. The man places his napkin beside his plate while he is standing to greet people stopping by the table. It's not thoughtful to "visit" too long at a table where people are dining and where a man must stand too long watching his own dinner get cold.

* When you know you're going to a fine restaurant, it's fun to study these French and Italian names for some of the food you like best. Once you know them, ordering from a menu will be a breeze.

Agneau (ann-yo)—lamb
A la mode (ah lah mowed)—with ice cream
Artichauts (art-ee-show)—artichokes
Asperges (as-perzj)—asparagus
Au beurre (oh burr)—with butter
Au gratin (ah grah-tan)—with cheese sauce
Au jus (oh zhu)—with gravy
Bifteck (beef-teck)—steak

Bisque (beesk)—cream fish soup
Boeuf (buff)—beef
Bombe (bome-buh)—molded frozen dessert or ice cream
Bouillon (boo-yon)—clear soup
Canard (can-arr)—duck
Champignons (shahm-pee-nyon)—mushrooms
Chou (shoo)—cabbage
Citron (see-tron)—lemon
Consommé (con-so-may)—clear soup
Côte (coat)—chop
Cotelette (coat-let)—cutlet
Crème (krem)—cream
Filet (fee-lay)—meat or fish without a bone in it
Foie (fwah)—liver
Fraises (frez)—strawberries
Froid (frwah)—cold
Fromage (fro-maj)—cheese
Gâteau (gah-toe)—cake
Glace (glahs)—jellied
Haricots verts (ah-ree-ko ver)—green string beans
Jambon (zjam-bone)—ham
Nouilles (noo-wee)—noodles
Oeufs (uff)—eggs
Patisserie (pah-tee-seuh-ree)—pastry and tarts
Pois (pwah)—green peas
Poisson (pwah-son)—fish
Pommes de terre (pum duh tair)—potatoes
Porc (pore)—pork
Potage (po-tahzj)—soup
Poulet (poo-lay)—chicken
Riz (ree)—rice
Roti (ro-tee)—roasted
Sauté (sew-tay)—fried
Vin (vanh)—wine

MOVIES, THEATERS, AND CONCERTS

When a girl goes to a movie with a boy, she stands in line with him unless the weather is so bad she's better off in the lobby until he has bought tickets. As she enters the theater she steps ahead of the boy and waits until he's handed over the tickets to the ticket-taker. If there is an usher, the girl goes down the aisle directly following the usher, and the boy follows. When there is no usher, the boy goes first to find good seats, then lets the girl enter the row first. When there are two couples, girls sit side by side with a boy to the left and right.

It's rude to come late to a play or a concert because there is only one performance each night, so that latecomers angling through rows like white hunters on a safari can truly disturb the audience. At a concert, wait until the entire musical selection is finished before applauding. At the end of the piece, the conductor will turn and bow, which is your cue to clap. If in doubt, wait for the rest of the audience to start. The other time for applause is when the conductor or orchestra leader first comes out on the stage at the beginning of the concert.

Traveling Alone

It's like getting your wings to set off alone on a bus, train, or plane. You feel very grown up as you kiss your parents goodbye and promise to call as soon as you get there. Most of the planning will have been done by your parents—and maybe an airline stewardess has been told to keep an eye on you—but you're still gloriously alone in the big world. So here are a few helpful hints:

* Take as few pieces of luggage as possible, particularly hand luggage which has to be flat enough to go under airline seats or you won't be permitted to board with it.

* Dress for comfort, of course, but neatly—not like a stowaway.

* Keep track of your tickets and schedule. Know how many stops the train or bus will make before it arrives at your destination; then you won't get the jitters if you doze off or get lost in a good book.

* Wear a watch so you don't have to ask what time it is every few minutes. If you don't own one, borrow one for the trip. Learn to calculate time in terms of the length of your trip. Find out how long it should be to get to Pittsburgh, Chicago, or wherever you're going; how long between major stops.

* Have emergency numbers in a small notebook—your mother or father's office number, for instance, plus the telephone number of the people you're visiting.

* Ask questions if you're worried or puzzled—from the bus driver, the train ticket collector, the stewardess—otherwise you'll be a basket case of nerves on arriving.

TRAVEL TIPPING—No one gets tipped on an airplane, bus, or train except when you travel on a sleeping car, and then your parents will tip the porter who made up your beds—at the end of the trip if they're with you, or in advance if you're traveling alone on a Pullman car. You tip porters who carry your luggage from a terminal or station to a taxi or car. Figure on 50¢ per bag as minimum. You tip a taxi driver a minimum of 25¢ tip for each part of a dollar on the meter. You don't have to tip in the snack bar of a terminal or station, but when you're a bit older and have enough time between changes to eat in the full-fledged restaurant of a

The Smithsonian Institution Washington DC

travel terminal, calculate 15 percent of the bill for your tip. Leave it beside your plate on the table, or on the little tray a waiter will sometimes use to hand you your bill.

* On long trips, take something to read, knit, embroider, or work at—time seems to go twice as slowly when you're among strangers, so plan to fill it.

House Guesting

When you're invited to a friend's house for more than an overnight slumber party—for a weekend in the country, for example, or even a whole week at a friend's farm or summer house—be sure your friend's parents "second" the invitation to one of your parents, not to you. It's exciting and a compliment to be invited to share another family's home but there are certain things you should know before you go.

* First of all, make sure when you're supposed to arrive and how long you'll be expected to stay. Get this straight before you leave home so that both families will know the plans. (If you're an overnight guest only, it's wise to leave or be picked up by noon the following day—it's much better to leave too soon than to linger around wearing out your welcome.)

* Take your own toilet necessities so you won't have to borrow anything. Pack your bag with what you usually reach for from morning till night—toothbrush, toothpaste, comb, curlers, hairbrush.

* Be prepared to do what your friend's family has planned, even if it isn't your favorite thing. And to follow their way of doing things, no matter how different it may be from your family's mealtime hours, TV time, bedtime. After all, it's fun to see how other people live—it might give you a new idea or two.

* Without being a fusspot, be neat when you are visiting as a house guest. Hang up your clothes, keep small items together—in your suitcase if there isn't drawer space— leave the bathroom clean (no ring around the tub, no hair in the basin, no wet towels on the floor). Make your own bed unless you've been told not to by your friend's *mother.*

* Don't raid the icebox or the kitchen every fifteen minutes. Strange, but starvation seems to set in the moment you're in an unfamiliar house; so when you feel pangs, say, "I feel hungry," or "Is there a little snack I can have?" No one wants you to wither away.

* Don't take up spying—prying into closets, opening drawers and bedroom doors.

* When you're ready to leave, pack up everything you brought so your hostess doesn't have to mail or deliver odds and ends you forgot.

* Thank your friend's mother before you leave. If you've been an overnight guest only, words are enough. If you've been a house guest for several days, write a thank-you note within two or three days after you return home. If you have stayed a week or more—during summer vacation, for instance—it is nice to send a little gift along with your note. You and your mother can select what your friend's mother might like.

When your friends are your house guests

If your friend is going to share your room, make space in the closet for her clothes and see that there are two or three empty hangers. In the bathroom, see that she has her own towel, washcloth, drinking glass.

If your friend is staying for several days, and especially if she is from another city or neighborhood, make some sort of program to entertain her, show her your city or neighborhood, and introduce her to some of your pals. You don't have to be a social director or a guest-watcher every minute, but you do have to realize a visitor gets bored doing nothing for days on end except talking.

P.S.: Even if it's only for an overnight stay, you must get your parents' permission before inviting a friend. Then stay around the house at the time she is expected to greet her and, if she's a new friend, to introduce her to your family. It can embarrass a visitor if she has to explain to your mother who she is and why she's there simply because you chose that hour to go bike riding or to the newsstand.

Letter Writing and Thank-You Notes

Have you been poking through the morning mail lately, hoping for a letter addressed to *you* for a change? If you're not getting enough mail, perhaps it's because you haven't been sending any out. A letter or a note means ten times as much as a telephone call, especially when you write amusingly and clearly. With so many attractive and inexpensive writing papers available—even in the supermarket and dime store—there's no reason for you to miss out on the pleasures of correspondence.

How to begin and end a letter

* Write your address at the upper right corner of the page—street and number on the top line, city and state on the second, and the date on a third line. Write out the month without abbreviating. No periods or commas are used at the ends of the lines. If your stationery is printed with name and/or address, you may add the date at the end of the letter slightly below your signature and flush with the left margin.

* Begin with the *salutation:* "Dear Mary," "Dear Grand-ma," "Hi, pal!"

* Keep even, wide margins on the left and right sides of the paper, and try to keep lines straight; otherwise your letter looks babyish.

* To close, write below the body of the letter and a little to the right of center: "Love," "Sincerely yours," "Fondly," "See you soon."

* When writing to someone you don't know personally, or to whom you are addressing a business letter, use a colon instead of a comma ("Dear Mr. Smith:") and close by writing "Yours truly" or "Sincerely yours," instead of too personal buddy-buddy wording.

* Even when you type a letter, always sign your name by hand.

How to address an envelope

* Center in three lines:

THE FULL NAME OF THE PERSON OR PERSONS ADDRESSED
THE FULL STREET NUMBER AND NAME
THE CITY, STATE, AND ZIP CODE

Omit punctuation at end of these lines. They may be in block form or slightly indented, but are always centered on envelope.

* Write your name and return address on the back of the envelope if it isn't printed there.

* "Mr.," "Mrs.," "Miss," or "Mr. and Mrs." should pre-cede the name of the person to whom you're writing except for a boy under 13 years old, who is addressed as "Master John Brown." From 13 to 18, no title is used for a boy. He becomes "Mr." at eighteen.

* When you write to two sisters, address the envelope
  "Misses Connie and Jennifer Jones." When you write to
  two brothers, use "Messrs. Joel and Dawson Smith"
  ("Messrs." is the abbreviation for the French word
  "Messieurs," which means "Misters").

* When the letter consists of two or three pages, put the first
  page on top followed by subsequent pages. Fold letter in
  half or in thirds (the bottom third up first, then the top
  third down over it). Insert the letter with the fold on top
  and the opening part of the letter next to the flap side of
  the envelope; this way when a letter is taken from the
  envelope it doesn't have to be turned around for reading.

* Place a stamp in the upper right corner of the envelope.
  Post offices now use electronic equipment to sort mail, so
  a misplaced stamp could hold up your letter for days.

THANK-YOU NOTES

Should be written within one week at most after your return home from being a house guest. If you have been a visitor in a friend's house for a weekend or longer, send a note to her mother or whoever was in charge of things (could be an aunt, grandmother, stepmother) thanking her for inviting you and showing you a good time.

For a gift you've received and liked

It's easy to rave about a gift you particularly wanted, but it's still necessary to mention what it was. Don't say, "Thank you for the gift," but do say, "Thank you for the charm bracelet (sweater, or whatever)," and tell what you intend to do with it: "I'm going to wear it tomorrow to the school dance."

For a gift you don't really like

Even if you have three just like it, or the gift is what you used to get when you were in second grade, stress thoughtfulness when you write your thank-you note: "It was nice of you to remember my 11th birthday, Aunt Kate" or "Even though I'm eleven now I still like plush animals . . ." (a hint you've outgrown a lot of standard gifts), then go on to a second topic such as what you did to celebrate your birthday.

* All thank-you notes should be written within seven days after you receive a gift. If you can't think of too much to say, ask your mother or father to add a P.S. to the note, and kill two birds with one shot.

"I Never Get Any Mail!"

"Why don't people ever write to *me* for a change?!?" No wonder you complain. Ever since you could block-print in capitals you've been writing nothing more than duty letters to thank grandparents and relatives for birthday and holiday gifts. But never an answer in return, as everybody knows. Cheer up—there are ways to start those cards and letters coming in.

Write to friends who've moved out of town or gone to different schools, to pals when you're at camp or on a trip with your family. Write to people you read about or listen to in the news—over television and radio, in magazines or daily papers. Write to members of the government, such as the mayor of your own town, when you have an opinion, a question, or even a complaint. If your letter is well thought out, you'll get an answer every time.

Keep an address book, starting with addresses and telephone numbers of your relatives (include your father's and mother's office addresses and telephone numbers). As your correspondence increases, that little book will be filled with friends who are just a letter away. On a dull day read through it until you come to the one person you'd like to "talk to" in writing.

For the three kinds of letter writing you'll be doing, here are some pointers:

* *Thank-you notes,* as we've already said, are written to people who send you gifts and to your hostess when you have been a house guest for a weekend or longer. A thank-you also goes to anyone who gives a party in your honor (although for the time being most parties given for you will be in your own home and, of course, you don't write thank-you letters to your family unless you like to see people fall down in a dead faint).

   "One-liner" thank-yous are not very satisfying, so mention a highlight of your visit, some special feature of a party. And if you're thanking someone for a gift, say something about it; otherwise it might seem you've forgotten exactly what was in the box.

* *Almost everyone learns to type these days* and you should, too. But reserve typing for business letters and school projects as much as possible. It's warmer and more personal to write invitations, acceptances, regrets, letters of congratulations, and thank-you notes by hand. Even when you start receiving formal or semi-formal invitations to weddings, proms, and debut dances, your acceptances and regrets should be written by hand in exactly these forms:

(ACCEPTANCE) Miss Jill Richards
accepts with pleasure
the kind invitation of
Mr. and Mrs. Thompson
on Saturday, the first of December,
at four o'clock

(REGRET)   Miss Jill Richards
                         regrets
             that because of a previous engagement
                 she will be unable to accept
                    Mr. and Mrs. Thompson's
                       kind invitation
                   for the first of December

LETTERS TO BUSINESS FIRMS
AND IMPORTANT PEOPLE

When writing to a business firm, say "Dear Sir:" or "Sirs:" (not "Gentlemen:" or "Dear Sirs:"). If the firm is made up of women, say "Dear Madam:" End business letters with "Sincerely yours," or just "Sincerely," then sign your full name—but never with "Miss" or "Mr." in front of it. There is one exception: If your name is a boy-or-girl one like Leslie add "(Mr.)" or "(Miss)" in parentheses so that the person answering your letter can address you correctly.

Any good-looking letter

* *Has a wide margin* at the top, bottom, and sides of the page.

* *Has the street address* on the top line, your city, state, and zip code on the second line and the full date (January 1, 1976) on the third line—all in a neat block formation at the upper right-hand corner of the page.

* *Is sent in a properly addressed envelope,* legibly handwritten or typed. For a personal letter, address the envelope with each line slightly indented; for a business letter, use a neat block style. Center the address on the envelope, whichever style you use, and omit punctuation at the ends of the lines. The name, street, city and state should be writ-

ten on separate lines, without abbreviations or initials except where initials are used in a business name. Be sure to include the zip code. If you don't know it, look it up in the Post Office directory—your letter will arrive at least one day earlier with a zip.

(EXAMPLE) Miss Martha Conway
1928 Hull Road
Vienna, Virginia 22180

* *Has a return address* on the back of the envelope or on the upper left-hand corner of the envelope. If it isn't printed there, write it yourself.

* *Has "Miss," "Mr.," or "Master"* before the name on the envelope. For a boy under 13, use "Master"; over 13, use "Mr." For any girl, use "Miss" before her name. (If you don't know whether a woman is married or not, you may use Ms.)

* *Has both your first and last name* in the signature at the end of the letter unless your name is so unusual (Hermione?) it can stand alone, or you have a regular and frequent correspondence going with the person you're writing to.

Addressing important people

A UNITED STATES OR STATE SENATOR
ENVELOPE ADDRESS: The Honorable James A. Lee
United States Senate
Washington, D. C. 20006
or
The Honorable James A. Lee
(Location of State Capitol)
Albany, New York (zip code)

LETTER OPENING: Dear Senator Lee:

110

CLOSING: Respectfully yours, *or* Sincerely yours,

A UNITED STATES OR STATE CONGRESSMAN
ENVELOPE ADDRESS: The Honorable Charles A. Lindsay
                    U. S. House of Representatives
                    Washington, D. C. 20006
                              or
                    The Honorable Charles A. Lindsay
                    (Name of State Capitol)
                    Des Moines, Iowa (zip code)

LETTER OPENING: Dear Mr. Lindsay:

LETTER CLOSING: Respectfully yours, *or* Sincerely yours,

A GOVERNOR
ENVELOPE ADDRESS: The Honorable Samuel E. Walsh
                    Governor of (State)
                    The Governor's Mansion
                    (City, state, zip code)

LETTER OPENING: Dear Governor Walsh:

LETTER CLOSING: Respectfully yours, *or* Sincerely yours,

A GOVERNOR AND HIS WIFE
ENVELOPE ADDRESS: The Honorable Samuel E. Walsh and
                    Mrs. Walsh

LETTER OPENING: Dear Governor and Mrs. Walsh:

A MAYOR
ENVELOPE ADDRESS: The Honorable John Jones
                    Mayor of Warren
                    City Hall
                    Warren, Pennsylvania (zip code)

LETTER OPENING: Dear Mayor Jones:

LETTER CLOSING: Respectfully yours, *or* Sincerely yours,

THE PRESIDENT OF THE UNITED STATES
ENVELOPE ADDRESS: The President
                   The White House
                   Washington, D. C. 20006

LETTER OPENING: Dear Mr. President: *or* Mr. President:

LETTER CLOSING: Respectfully, *or* Very respectfully,

THE PRESIDENT'S WIFE
ENVELOPE ADDRESS: Mrs. Ford (note: no first name, hers or
                   the President's)
                   The White House
                   Washington, D. C. 20006

LETTER OPENING: Dear Mrs. Ford:

LETTER CLOSING: Sincerely yours,

THE PRESIDENT AND HIS WIFE
ENVELOPE ADDRESS: The President and Mrs. Ford

LETTER OPENING: Dear President and Mrs. Ford:

LETTER CLOSING: Respectfully, *or* Very respectfully,

A CATHOLIC PRIEST
ENVELOPE ADDRESS: The Reverend John Jones
                   Our Lady of Fatima
                   Scarsdale, New York (zip code)

LETTER OPENING: Dear Father Jones:

LETTER CLOSING: Faithfully yours,

A RABBI

ENVELOPE ADDRESS: Dr. J. A. Jones *or* Rabbi J. A. Jones

LETTER OPENING: Dear Dr. Jones: *or* Dear Rabbi Jones:

LETTER CLOSING: Yours sincerely,

A PROTESTANT MINISTER

ENVELOPE ADDRESS: The Reverend John Jones *or* The Reverend Dr. John Jones

LETTER OPENING: Dear Mr. Jones: *or* Dear Dr. Jones:

LETTER CLOSING: Faithfully yours, *or* Sincerely yours,

PERSONAL CORRESPONDENCE IS THE MOST REWARDING

When you write a chatty letter using words and thoughts you'd express if you were actually talking to that person, you'll get an answer—it's guaranteed!

Here's another plus: You can learn to analyze your friends' handwriting in order to better understand their personalities. No two people have the same handwriting, just as no two people have the same fingerprints. You can develop a fascinating skill by studying some character traits found in handwriting. Keep in mind there is nothing "bad" in handwriting analysis—it is just a *key* to someone's personality. Following are a few indications from *Scriptease*, a book written by Renée C. Martin, who is an expert in this scientific field (she has often helped solve court cases by matching handwriting characteristics on documents, checks, and even memos).

Handwriting that slants to the right

Handwriting Consult—
199 Nassau St
Princeton NJ 08540

Indicates a person is secure, adaptable to people, and able to communicate freely.

Handwriting that slants to the left

Mr. Kramer I wish to thank both for the console

Means the writer has a non-conformist attitude, a fear of being hurt, and, therefore, a fear of communicating in any way that might leave him vulnerable.

Handwriting that is perpendicular

By virtue of my academic
in both metallurgy

Indicates a writer who weighs every action, reaction, and emotion.

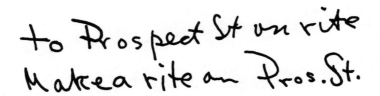

Means that person is undecided as to how openly he wants to express himself. If a single word is at a different angle from the others, that word is in some way special to the writer.

Capital "I's"

The capital "I" indicates a writer's feelings about *himself*. If it is *slanted to the left in an otherwise right-slanted handwriting,* it reveals a self-critical nature.

LEFT-SLANT CAPITAL I

If it is *slanted to the right in an otherwise perpendicular or left-slanted handwriting,* it shows selfishness.

RIGHT-SLANT CAPITAL I

A *capital "I" that is larger than other capitals* indicates the writer's self-esteem or pride in himself. One that is *smaller* denotes humility.

LARGE CAPITAL I

> I was at the doctors off yesterday and he said I was perfectly allright

A *capital "I" made with a loop* tells of the writer's self-involvement. The farther left the horizontal stroke goes, the farther back in the writer's past lies a traumatic experience he has never been able to completely forget.

LOOPED I WITH LEFT HORIZONTAL

The more open a capital "I" is (without any cross strokes), the more considerate the writer is of others.

AN OPEN CAPITAL I

> rung I had a
> e getting a Cub
> ter. — Finally I

A *printed capital "I"* shows intelligence, maturity, flexibility, and a clear, honest self-image. If there are *two horizontal strokes* on the printed "I," the writer has an accurate appraisal of himself and limits himself to his capabilities.

I hope I am one of many   PRINTED CAPITAL I

not sure yet. I can

a course that I have taken

I can't audit a course that

PRINTED CAPITAL I WITH HORIZONTALS

P.S.: *Printing instead of writing* is not babyish. In fact, the most intelligent people print their messages because they are usually people who really want to communicate. So there goes another generation gap!

Capital letters

The way capital letters are formed has a lot to say about the writer. Capitals that are *taller* than the ones you learned in school indicate exaggerated self-confidence.

(TALLER)

Capitals that are wider than the regular school form are made by talkative individuals.

(WIDER)

Flowery, ornate capitals in an otherwise average handwriting show the writer's desire to impress others with his artistic ability and taste. He may even be "putting on airs."

(FLOWERY, ORNATE)

Capital letters at a different angle from the rest of the writing show that the writer's surface personality is different from his true self.

Easy-to-read handwriting

Shows the writer's desire to be understood by others.

EASY-TO-READ WRITING

Difficult-to-read handwriting

Indicates a person who is more interested in what *he* or *she* thinks than in what the reader may think. He may in fact be a non-listener, period.

> I just put up a Window Rut
> for my Television Set and if
> lucky it doesn't fall dow

DIFFICULT-TO-READ WRITING

Extremely illegible handwriting

Indicates an antisocial personality. Of course, legibility —like beauty—may often be in the eye of the beholder. In other words, you have to want to read what someone writes you.

Signatures

Signatures show the surface personality of a writer. So even when you receive typed letters you can determine a bit about the writer by the way he signs his name.

When a writer makes a *flourish in his signature,* he wants to be recognized and appreciated.

An *underline "crossed" by two lines* shows concern with money.

If the signature is larger than the rest of the writing in the letter, the writer likes to appear self-confident and indifferent to details.

LARGE SIGNATURE

If the signature is smaller than the main body of the writing, he is trying to give the impression he is interested in details.

SMALL SIGNATURE

If a signature is perpendicular while the rest of the letter is written with a distinct right or left slant, the writer wants to give an impression of control and intellectuality but he is really quite emotional.

John Smith　　PERPENDICULAR SIGNATURE

Dots over "i's"

These are good keys to people, too. *The more precisely the dot over the "i" is positioned,* the more attention the writer gives to detail. *Absence of a dot over an "i"* shows either forgetfulness or a lack of interest in details. *The higher the dot over the "i,"* the more imaginative a writer is. *A circle dot over an "i"* means the writer is creative. There's one exception: If the rest of the writing is rather ordinary, the circle-dot means he's faking or affecting his artistic nature.

You can read more about handwriting in *Scriptease* by Renée C. Martin (New Hope Publishing, paperback, $2.00.)

School—
One–third of Your Life

These are your green years, your in-between, soon-to-be-teen years. So you're in the best part of your life. You're really and truly growing.

Your days are pretty much wrapped up with school, which takes one-third of your life. You sleep eight hours, school takes eight hours one way or another, and that leaves eight hours for doing the hundreds of things that interest you outside of school.

Now is the time to plan a few goals, look forward to high school, take stock of yourself and the direction in which you hope to go.

If you're new in school or in the neighborhood

There are definite and helpful things you can do—or face up to—to make yourself feel at home fast:

* *It's a fact*—nothing is more exciting to a class than a new face, so be prepared for open stares or guarded glances. One way or another you'll be given the once-over by everyone in the room.

* *Proceed with caution* as you begin this new part of your life. Sometimes it's best to bide your time until the newness of everything wears off. You'll become confused if you try to be chummy with everyone at once. There's also another danger: If you're too quick to fall in with the first people who warm up to you, you may later find them the last people on earth you want to pal around with. Wait.

* *Smile and put on a cheerful expression* that will put you and your classmates at ease until you get your bearings.

* *Try to find out (or ask your family to discover)* if some of your classmates live near you so you can meet them at the bus stop and ask some questions about the school routine and your teachers even before you get there. If you can't do the locating yourself, the school principal's office has this information and will give it to your parents over the phone.

* *If you have to go cold turkey to a new school* try to stay calm and quiet within yourself even if you feel like turning and running at the sight of the new school—or your new house. You may not believe this, but every new experience, painful as it may seem, helps you to mature and grow up. It's by weathering change and adjusting to it that we gain self-confidence.

* *When you've found your first new friends* you may be tempted to show how relieved and grateful you are by becoming a carbon copy of them—by copying their accent, vocabulary, clothes, even their pet hates. You can admire your new friends and even improve yourself by studying them, but don't feel you have to do a complete character transfusion in order to be liked. In fact, maybe they will want to improve themselves by studying *you.*

* *Loneliness can set in.* No matter how busy or happy you are, you're bound to have unexpected periods of loneliness when you least expect them. This feeling of loneliness is even more difficult to cope with when you belong to a big family or have made a lot of new friends. You think, "Why do I feel so lonely?" You wonder if you're unappreciative of your friends or disloyal to your family.

Many times a down-in-the-dumps feeling can be cured by a good night's sleep, a long walk, a call or letter to the good friend you've missed since you've moved, or by doing a favor for someone else just to get your mind off yourself.

Then sometimes—at the opposite end of this problem—your feeling of loneliness is genuine; you *are* new in town and you have exactly zero friends. Moving from place to place is a very real trauma. In the U.S. today the average family moves once every three years. Sometimes, if a father is with the government or the military, a moving van in the driveway is as common as a station wagon in front of a suburban house.

* *If you can't lick loneliness—or its first cousin, boredom—*use it to develop hobbies and your own talents. This is the time to use whatever skills you have to fill your own spare time and to make friends with others who have the same interests. If you're good at sports and games, fine; you'll find it easy to get acquainted with others. But if you're not a specialist in those areas, break the ice by going to a hobby shop or a pet store. No matter how weird your interest is—from collecting butterflies to raising snakes —you'll find at least one person there who's into the same subject. And ta-da! you've found a friend. If you're learning to sew, shop for remnants and new fabrics in the local stores, look through the new easy-to-make styles in the pattern books. Before you know it someone your age will be asking you which dress you think would be better for her to try making. Next step is usually sewing together at your house or hers—and it's goodbye loneliness.

If You Think Your Parents Are Still in the Dark Ages

Most people in your age group begin to believe that their parents don't know anything and that their friends' parents are the only ones who know what's going on. What's strange is that your friends may think YOUR parents are the only ones who aren't square.

This is natural. Make the most of it.

If you don't want to discuss things like drugs, boys, dates, wearing make-up, or love with your own parents, go to whichever of your friends' parents you feel will be the most understanding. Ideally, it would be nice if you could have that same kind of relationship with your own parents, but sometimes you can't. That's because there is a tendency on the part of most parents NOT to want to believe you know things about the facts of life or anything controversial. They're trying to blind themselves to what you're facing up to. Why? Because they're afraid for you. So their reasoning is this: "Maybe if I don't talk or think about that, it will go away."

You, on the other hand, must find out. First, try your

questions out on your own family, but if they don't respond, talk to a teacher, an advisor, or, as previously suggested, to someone else's parents you admire and trust. You'll be amazed at how non-emotional grown-ups are when their own children are not involved.

You're at an age when you want to assert yourself. Often you're just testing, trying to find out what your parents actually think. You provoke them; they say "No," and you're almost glad that they do. You pull back—until the next time. The problem lies in the tension caused by your testing, their getting angrier and angrier with each new probe, and all because of the things they've been reading in the papers, seeing on TV and in the movies that scare them into predicting bad things for you.

For example: you're having a party and someone turns out all the lights. Some parents may think the worst, and turn the lights back on. If this happens with your parents, you'll be irritated because you've been embarrassed in front of your friends. But a part of you will be relieved. Your parents have just taken the responsibility off your back for what might actually have gotten out of hand anyway.

When your mother works (outside the home as well as inside)

Sometimes mothers have to get jobs whether they like it or not. Then again some mothers work when their children are all in school because they want to be part of the outside world, or because they're picking up a career they had to drop when they were married and you came into the picture. In either case, when there is a mother who has a job outside of homemaking, you need to be aware of certain things.

You have to understand and get straight why she is

working, what she is doing, and what hours she works. You'll be proud of her and what she is accomplishing when you understand a little about it, even if she works a complicated computer.

You must help out at home—set the table, defrost a steak, take telephone messages, keep track of your own house key in case your mother or father must work late and gets home after you do.

Keep your mother's office telephone number—your father's, too—in your wallet and in your address book in case of an emergency at school or home.

Make sensible use of the time you spend with your mother. You don't see her as often as you would if she stayed at home all day so it's difficult to get in the habit of remembering what it was you wanted to tell or ask her, but this will come with practice. Your mother is aware of her double responsibilities so she can still help you remember that you have a test in two weeks—she'll remind you of it, or of the library book you have to return—if you'll share with her and let her know you need her help.

Divorce Isn't the End of the World

We are now living in a world that is not as simple as it used to be, a world where many of your friends will come from divorced families. They will be living with a stepmother or just a father or just a mother. You have to be kind about this because your friends will never admit that they feel a little different. Sometimes they're angry and they behave in odd ways. Try to understand them; don't hold it against them. If they want to talk about it, listen; they're trying to say something about their feelings toward their parents and family. But don't pry if you sense they're too embarrassed to discuss the issues.

If divorce hits your own family remember it wasn't your fault and you shouldn't feel guilty about it. You had nothing to do with it; it was a problem between your parents.

What you have to do is adjust to the situation. You may feel slightly out of place, but today in the U.S. there is so much divorce that people don't consider it a mark of disgrace.

It's very important when you feel there's something wrong about your parents' relationship, or when your friends make something weird out of it, that you talk to someone, preferably someone who knows and cares about your family—your mother or father, an aunt, your grandmother, or a long-time family friend. You'll be pleasantly surprised: when you bring a grown-up problem to a grown-up person he'll treat you as more grown up.

If you want to read more about the matter of divorce, there is an excellent book called *What Shall We Tell the Kids?* by Dr. Bennett Olshaker (Dell paperback, $1.50) in which divorce, separation, remarriage, and single-parent homes are all explained from both the parents' and the children's point of view.

What to Do When Your Family Is "Different"

Every family seems to have a problem it wishes would just go away. It may be a nuisance problem only. Perhaps your father is a fireman so sometimes he sleeps all day because he's been fire-fighting all night, which means you have to whisper until he wakes up. Or it may be a much more serious problem: your mother is an alcoholic, your grandparent is senile and lives with you, your brother is retarded, or someone in your household is a helpless cripple.

You may have lived with the problem all your life, paying no attention to it until now, when suddenly you feel it cramping your style and giving you the jitters about bringing your friends home. One girl whose mother drinks too much makes up new lies every time a friend says, "I've never seen your room; what's it like?" She panics and says she's lost her house key, or that her room is being painted, the whole house is being painted, the house is on fire, this isn't really her house.

Some of your problems may be incurable; most are not. Many will pass. Several may be the same as your friends' problems, but they're as frightened as you are.

132

Don't think everything is your fault or that because you've done something wrong you've brought on the disaster. If you sense a new problem when you come home from school, ask someone about it right away: "Why is Dad acting that way?" Your mother may say, "It has nothing to do with you; he's afraid he may lose his job," or "He's worried about being transferred to a new city." If the problem is one you know you're going to have to live with, find someone older to talk it over with. Ask about the problem: What is it? Why is it? Is it going to end? Is there anything I can do to help?

If a family member or neighbor or long-time family friend can't answer your questions, there is plenty of outside help for almost any problem:

* Alateen is for children of alcoholic parents; there's a branch of it in almost every community.

* School counselors, people at the YWCA and YMCA, and community action groups are waiting for you to take the first step, which is to ask for help.

Trouble gets doubled when you try to handle it yourself because you lack the maturity and judgment to solve problems that may have existed before you were born.

One exception: sometimes the problem *is* you. When you ask why everyone is so mean to you, you may hear this: "You've been pretty hard to get along with lately, and we'd like to know what your problem is." Then tell it.

Boy-Girl Talk

You're lucky to be living at a time when people are much more willing to talk about sex. Nowadays, when young people want to talk about it, grown-ups treat them very seriously. It's not a big deal anymore and abundant information is available in books you can get from school or the public library. It would take a whole book to talk about sex in your age group. We can only say that each person is different. Some girls menstruate earlier than others; some boys develop before other boys do. If you want to know more about the subject, these books are recommended because they deal with sex in more detail:

Facts Aren't Enough by Marion O. Lerrigo, American Medical Association, Chicago, 1962.

Understanding Sex by Lester A. Kirkendall, Science Research Associates, Chicago, 1947.

What Teenagers Want To Know by Florence Levinsohn and Kelly G. Lombard, Budlong Press Company, Chicago, 1962.

Approaching Adulthood by Marion O. Lerrigo and Helen Southard, American Medical Association, Chicago, 1961.

For Youth To Know (Adolescent problems; human reproduction) by Donald A. Boyer, Laidlaw Brothers, River Forest, Ill., 1966.

Also, some schools now have sex education material available for you to take home and study. Obviously, there will be a certain amount of joking about sex in your age group, but don't think you're square because you *need to know more* about sex than is available at the local snack bar or whispered about during a slumber party.

Boys vs. Girls

vs.

Boys vs. Help!

Boys need to be treated very delicately. It's not their fault that their emotional development is slower than that of girls. Sometimes they test out two or three years behind girls.

But it all evens out in the long run because many older men seem to look younger than women their age—as if nature subtracts from the beginning and adds to the end in order to give men surplus strength for more responsibility.

Once a girl knows this fact, she can begin to understand some puzzlers. Example: the boy who is *the* boy all the girls in the class have a crush on. Does that boy know it? Of course he does.

Then why doesn't he choose just one girl? Because he likes his role and he knows there's safety in numbers until he can cope with a one-girl relationship.

Why does he pretend—and even declare—that he hates all girls? Because it works; that's what got him where he is today—at the top of the list.

Why does he tease and provoke girls, then run the other

way if any one of them gets too close? Teasing, provoking, and running take the place of words until the "Me Tarzan, you Jane" in him finds a better way to communicate.

Since *the* boy will stay out of reach for a while, let's look at boys as a group to see what they are running from.

WHAT BOYS DON'T LIKE ABOUT GIRLS—AND THE OTHER WAY AROUND

Boys don't like

Girls who are bossy.
Girls who are too clinging.
Girls who exaggerate.
Girls who gossip and tattle; who are too nosy.
Girls who beat them regularly at games. (This is probably against all Women's Lib teaching, but it's true.)
Girls who hang around when they're told they're not wanted.
Girls who put on airs, act like princesses, think they're so ravishing everyone ought to swoon over them.
Girls who are too demanding when it comes right down to dollars and cents—choosing the most expensive banana split, first-run movie, best place to meet or eat.
Girls who don't keep promises; who agree to meet a boy then don't show up.
Girls who name-, place-, and price-drop.

Girls don't like

Boys who are so sloppy and dirty (hair, fingernails, feet, sweater) that they actually have unpleasant odors.
Boys who make fun of them—their braces, their hairdo, their brothers and sisters.

Boys who brag too much.

Boys who show off with money.

Boys who make a big deal about what they own or what their parents own.

Boys who put girls down—their fat legs, their height.

Why all of the above? NOBODY LIKES TO BE HURT BY SOMEBODY ELSE.

How to
Manage Money

Except for your allowance, money you may get for helping around the house, and gifts from relatives, you're not going to have much money of your own for a while yet. But this is still a good time to start learning where money goes, how much things cost, and how you want to save or spend your own money.

Know what your allowance covers

At first it may be too small to take care of much more than a comic book, candy bar, or dime-store purchases each week. But as you become more responsible, your family will be proud to enlarge your allowance to cover bus fares, movies, even clothing items, your pet's needs, books, or music.

Open a savings account

You can have one at any age. To open a savings account at the bank you will need your Social Security number, which can be obtained by writing to the Bureau of Internal Revenue, Washington, D. C. And your account must be "under the control of" one of your parents until you are 18 years old. You can deposit savings by yourself as soon as you learn how to fill out a deposit slip available at the bank. But in most states you cannot withdraw any savings without your parent's signature on the withdrawal slip until you're 18. Savings earn interest, and the bank sends you a statement at regular intervals to tell you how your money has grown.

"JUNIOR CAREER GIRLS" EARN EXTRA MONEY EARLY

Because of school work and special lessons, you'll be limited to part-time "mini jobs" for now, but there are plenty of them.

Baby-sitting

This is to girls what a paper route is to a boy. You should be in your twelfth year before taking on the responsibility of baby-sitting, but here are some pointers to help you establish a regular list of customers:

1. Ask the parents exactly what they want you to do for the baby while you're in charge. What do you feed him, and when? What time does he have to go to bed? Are you expected to give the baby his bath?
2. Ask the parents where they can be reached by telephone while they are gone—just in case. Then write down the telephone number, or if the parents are going to a public place, its name at least. And settle on what

time they will be home so you can tell your own parents
when to expect you.

3. Pay attention to the baby, play games, have patience,
but when you sense you're overdoing it, learn how to
say, "That's enough of that for now." Baby-sitting
should be more than just the indoor survival test some

toddlers seem to have in mind. And remember that overstimulating games, jokes, romps just before bedtime are not recommended for small-fry.

4. Stay awake until the parents come home. Ask permission to use the TV, but keep it low so that you can hear baby sounds from the bedroom.

5. If there is more than one toddler, bring a friend with you the first few times at least. You'll have to split your earnings, but write it off as insurance.

6. Know from the start how much you are going to earn per hour. The best way is to get the amount settled when your neighbor calls and asks if you care to baby-sit. You can say very nicely, "I'll be glad to. I charge 75¢ an hour. Is that all right with you?" Then there will be no disappointments at the end of a hard night's work.

7. Never spank or punish children for whom you're baby-sitting. You can say, "No," and give directions, but most parents resent punishment by an outsider, especially a young person.

8. Don't tie up the telephone. Lots of parents call in from time to time, particularly when you're a pre-teenager, and they get hysterical if the line is busy; they immediately picture their baby alone and in danger.

9. Don't raid the refrigerator, even if the baby's mother has said, "Help yourself if you're hungry." A cookie, a Coke, a glass of milk—fine. But don't feel you should stock up just because the food is there.

Pet-sitting

When your neighbors go on vacation, offer to take care of their pets. Feed them, walk them, even board them in your own house if you have your parents' permission and the space to pen the pets so they won't run away. Advice: demand that any animal you "sit" be housebroken.

Garage sales

Early spring and fall are perfect times to round up unwanted but salable items from your own attic or garage and from your neighbors' storage closets. Put a notice on the bulletin board at school or at the local drugstore, enlist a few friends to share the work (and the profits), then sell them from your own garage on a certain specified Sales Day. Or offer them for sale house-to-house, offering a few items at a time. Seller keeps one third of the sale price, with the remaining two thirds going to the original owner.

Lawn bazaars

They require more help and planning, but they're a whole day's fun—and often remarkably profitable. You and your best friends decide on competitive games such as horseshoes, ring toss, knocking down the most bottles with a tennis ball, darts, pinning the tail on the donkey, guessing the number of beans in a jar, drawing a lucky number from a hatful of folded numbered slips for a really good prize you must furnish, egg races, potato bag races, croquet, etc. Then set up a booth or a location for each game, with a poster telling the price for each "try." Other booths could consist of home-made brownies for sale, usable toys or games you want to sell, pots of herbs you've planted from seeds, paintings, drawings, photographs, or crafts you have created for sale. Each booth should be gaily decorated and have a sign identifying it and the prices of the merchandise. Let your parents help you with pricing. Sometimes neigh-

144

bors are too nice and will actually let their children hand over a dollar for that broken 29¢ toy you've overpriced.

Balloons are great attention-getters when you tie them to tables and booths; they attract passers-by in the neighborhood and they build good will, especially if you make it known that everyone who buys from your bazaar will be given a free balloon to take home.

Selling lemonade

It's fun and exciting, and your mother will undoubtedly be delighted with the idea. But figure it out: there's very little profit—and perhaps a loss—involved when you consider that all your ingredients have been furnished by your parents. The main value is practice in making change, sign painting, and stand decoration, plus a basic lesson in salesmanship and optimism.

Summer nursery school

You and at least one other girl or boy can open a summer day school for little tots. Two to three hours every morning or afternoon are sufficient because small children tire easily. Limit yourselves to the number of children you can supervise and entertain; set an hourly price that takes care of crayons, construction paper, games, balls, supplies you will need. Ask mothers to deliver and pick up their children from your house so you won't have to go crazy getting them home on time.

Breeding tropical fish

Buy an aquarium and one or two rare fish varieties,

then sell the offspring. You could also sell fish food from a stock you will have to invest in. Offshoot of this idea: advertise your services to clean aquariums around the neighborhood. It's a job everybody hates to do once the novelty has worn off.

Giving summer lessons

Give lessons to younger children—reading, writing, or any special talent you have in the world of music, art, dancing. You may not be an expert but the few years of lessons you've had will be more than adequate for a total beginner.

Indoor and outdoor chores

Every house in the neighborhood has seasonal or weekly jobs they would gladly pay someone else to do —garage cleaning, sidewalk sweeping, leaf raking, snow shoveling, garden weeding, car washing, silver polishing. Talk it over with your parents before you set the price per hour or per job, and they'll give you an idea of how much the traffic will bear.

It's Party Time!

Good parties are not born, they are created. Sometimes pulling a party together is as much fun as the event itself, especially when some of your best friends come over to help.

Until now, your parents have taken care of all details for your birthday parties, slumber parties, simple dinners. But you're old enough now to do most of the planning and preparation yourself.

Here are the basic steps and ingredients that produce such a good party you'll enjoy it as much as your guests do.

1. *First get permission* from your family to have the party. Ask a few days in advance—not the night before—and talk about the number of guests you'd like to invite, the food you'd like to serve, the room you'll need for the setting.
2. *Make a guest list.* If it's a small party, don't talk about it at school because you could hurt a lot of feelings. When you're allowed to invite your whole class, a guest list is still a good idea—you can show it to your parents to

147

refresh their memories on your classmates' names and use it yourself to check off acceptances and regrets.

3. *Send out invitations* by word of mouth, by telephone, or by mail. Make the invitations yourself, using your imagination, craft or construction paper, decals, and colored felt pens. Or if you're not up to it, buy them. But mail them about one week before the party. Invitations should specify:

 * *The type of party it is, especially if it's a birthday.*

 * *The date and time of the party.*

 * *Your full name, address, and telephone number*—particularly the telephone number so that your friends can RSVP, which means letting you know whether or not they can come. These initials are an abbreviation for the original French request: "Répondez, s'il vous plâit" (Respond, if you please).

 * *A map, drawn by you and enclosed* with the invitation, if your house is hard to find or if you've just moved.

4. *Wait for acceptances.* Have a couple of substitutes in mind in case some of your friends can't accept your invitation, but never let the substitute know he or she was second choice. If you've invited people by telephone, be prepared for last-minute calls about time, address, clothes, etc.—some people don't get things straight over the phone.

5. *Be dressed and ready to receive guests* a few minutes before party time so that you can answer the door. Until you are a full teenager, your mother is really the hostess and will stand beside you at the door to greet your friends. Your first duty as each guest arrives is to introduce her or him to your mother.

6. *Guests may bring gifts* if it's your birthday but don't stare at their hands to see if they're empty or gift-laden. Sometimes a friend will forget a gift and you don't want to give the impression she was invited just for the loot.

   When a friend brings a gift, accept it from her, say, "Thank you," and put it with other gifts to be opened all at once—it's more fun for the crowd that way. Whatever the gift, show appreciation even if you have one just like it or you think it's so silly that you're planning to give it to your kid sister tomorrow.

7. *Make a list of what must be done before the party.* Beginning with the menu—even if it's very simple, like Cokes, M & M's, and potato chips—list what you and your family plan to serve your guests. Your mother will do the necessary food shopping and most of the cooking, but you can go with her to see how quantities are calculated, and you can also help with the cooking.

   * *If it's a sit-down party,* help set the table, arrange flowers as a centerpiece for the table (keep them low so people can see over them), add candles, place cards, and favors if you are going to give them.

   * *If you're giving a slumber party,* plan where everyone will sleep and line up extra blankets and pillows even if your invitations specified "Bring your own sleeping bag." It's also important to let your friends know exactly what time the slumber party will start and whether it's before or after dinner. Even if you serve dinner, you'll find that slumber party guests eat on and off until very late at night.

Here are some good things to make and serve to hungry guests.

FABULOUS FUDGE

4½ cups sugar
1 can (14½-ounce size) evaporated milk
½ teaspoon salt
¼ pound butter or margarine
6 squares (each square equals 2 ounces) sweetened chocolate
2 cups chopped pecans or walnuts
2 packages (6-ounce size) semi-sweet chocolate bits
1 jar (7-ounce size) marshmallow creme
1 teaspoon vanilla

DIRECTIONS:

In a saucepan, combine sugar, milk, salt, and butter. Bring to a boil. Cook 5 minutes, stirring constantly. Remove from fire and add remaining ingredients, stirring until chocolate is melted and everything is well blended. Pour into 2 buttered pans (9 × 9 × 2-inch size). Chill until firm. Makes about 4 pounds.

SOFT, CHEWY BROWNIES MADE IN ONE PAN

This recipe is not only delicious but easy because you make the brownies on top of the stove using only one pan.

⅓ cup butter or margarine
2 squares unsweetened chocolate
1 cup sugar
1 teaspoon vanilla
2 eggs
¼ teaspoon salt
¾ cup sifted flour
½ cup chopped nuts

DIRECTIONS:

In a medium-sized saucepan, put ⅓ cup of butter or margarine and 2 squares of unsweetened chocolate. Melt them slowly over very low heat, stirring constantly so they don't burn. Remove from stove, cool a bit, then add 1 cup of regular sugar, 1 teaspoon of vanilla, 2 eggs (one at a time, stirring after each egg), ¼ teaspoon salt, and ¾ cup of sifted flour. Blend well, then add ½ cup chopped nuts and stir them so they're evenly distributed in the batter. Pour into an 8×8×2-inch pan which you've already buttered and dusted with flour. Bake for 30 or 35 minutes in a 350-degree oven. Cut into squares and sprinkle lightly with powdered sugar. Makes 16 yummy brownies.

SUGAR COOKIES (Buttery, crispy, the all-time favorite recipe)

1 cup butter or margarine
1¼ cups sugar
4 egg yolks, beaten
1 teaspoon baking soda
1 teaspoon cream of tartar
2 cups flour
1 teaspoon vanilla

DIRECTIONS:

Cream butter and sugar together (with electric mixer if you have one); add egg yolks and mix well. Combine baking soda, cream of tartar, and flour, and add to cookie mixture; add vanilla and blend thoroughly with a wooden or heavy spoon (never use mixer for this part). Roll into a ball, wrap in waxed paper, and place in refrigerator overnight—or if you forgot to start the night before, all day long. Break off pieces the size of large marbles; flour your hands and roll balls between palms. Place on cookie sheet 1 inch apart and bake in 375-degree oven about 10 minutes or until lightly brown. Makes about 48 cookies.

BUTTERSCOTCH BROWNIES (For non-chocolate eaters)

4 tablespoons melted butter or margarine
1 cup dark brown sugar
1 egg
½ teaspoon salt
¾ cup flour
1 teaspoon baking powder
½ teaspoon vanilla
¼ cup coconut
½ cup broken walnuts or pecans

DIRECTIONS:

Mix all ingredients together and spread in a buttered $8 \times 8 \times 2$-inch square pan. Bake at 350 degrees for 25 minutes. Cool and sprinkle with powdered sugar—or if you want to make super-delicious brownies, spread with this icing:

CARAMEL ICING

½ cup butter or margarine
½ cup brown sugar
¼ cup milk or half-and-half
1¾ to 2 cups powdered sugar
1 teaspoon maple extract or vanilla

DIRECTIONS:

Melt butter until brown, add sugar and cook, stirring, until sugar is completely melted. Pour in milk and stir. Cool. Add powdered sugar and extract; beat until thick enough to spread.

THE BEST HOT FUDGE SAUCE IN THE WORLD

½ cup cocoa
1 cup sugar
1 cup light Karo corn syrup
½ cup light cream or evaporated milk
¼ teaspoon salt
3 tablespoons butter
1 teaspoon vanilla

DIRECTIONS:

Combine all ingredients except vanilla in a saucepan. Cook over medium heat, stirring constantly, until the mixture comes to a rolling boil. Boil briskly 3 minutes, stirring occasionally. (If you've used too small a saucepan, mixture will boil over onto the stove, so start with a medium-sized one and you'll be safe.) Remove from heat and add vanilla. Serve warm. Can be stored in refrigerator and reheated next time—and it gets even thicker.

GRILLED HAM AND CHEESE SANDWICHES

First, butter two slices of bread the usual way and place a slice of cheese and a slice of ham between them. After you have put the sandwich together, butter the outside of each slice. (It's easier if you've let the butter soften before you start.) Put the sandwich in a warmed frying pan over low heat, and lay a small plate on top of it to weigh the sandwich down and hasten the melting of the cheese. In a few minutes, lift an edge of the bottom slice with a spatula or a pancake turner. If the bread is a golden brown, turn the sandwich and do the other side. Delicious.

WITH EGGS YOU'RE SUDDENLY A SUPER CHEF OMELETS ARE EASY, INEXPENSIVE AND SENSATIONAL-LOOKING

Some people make a big deal about omelets, but they're really one of the simplest dishes you can prepare in a hurry —and everyone loves eggs. Any 8- or 9-inch skillet will do as long as it's clean and dry. Two or three eggs make a better omelet than one, says Helen Corbitt, one of Texas's most famous cooks. Melt 2 tablespoons of butter in the pan; swivel it around so that the bottom and sides are coated. Beat the eggs lightly (using a fork) with ½ teaspoon salt and 1 tablespoon cold water or milk, then pour into the hot pan. Butter should be sizzling. Cook at high heat. As the omelet begins to cook, swirl it with the fork and pull edges of the mixture toward center of the pan. The runny part will fill the space. Repeat until all of the egg is cooked, but still soft. If you want to add anything like jelly, cheese, mushrooms, bits of ham, or crisp bacon, do it at this point. Then, with a spatula, fold two sides of the omelet toward the center of the pan and lift the pan so the omelet slides onto the plate. Serve and eat at once; nothing worse than cold eggs.

SCRAMBLED EGGS FOR A RAVENOUS CROWD

6 eggs
½ cup milk

½ teaspoon salt
3 tablespoons butter

DIRECTIONS:

Break eggs into a bowl; add milk and salt. Mix lightly with a fork or a whisk (not with an egg-beater or an electric blender or they'll be heavy and leathery)—just enough to break up the eggs. Melt butter in skillet. Pour in eggs and cook over moderate heat, stirring with a wooden spoon as eggs coagulate. As soon as they take shape, remove from heat and serve. Scrambled eggs should be a bit moist.

SOMETHING EXTRA: Mix ¼ cup grated or shredded cheese with eggs before you cook them; save a few pinches to scatter on top as you serve eggs.

P.S.: If cooking appeals to you, two of the best beginner books are *Look, I Can Cook* by Angela Burdick (American Heritage Press, $4.95) and *The Cookalong Book* by Barbara Wyden (McKay, $6.95).

8. *When you're planning a large party,* ask some of your best friends to be on a "house committee." One girl can take gifts and put them in a certain place, another girl can take coats or show guests where to put them, perhaps a third friend can keep, an eye on the living room—to introduce newcomers and keep conversation going while you're still at the front door.

9. *When someone new comes to a big party,* introduce her to the group at large, saying, "This is Pamela Jones, everybody," but don't just walk away and leave her. Take her over to one or two friends and introduce her again so she'll have someone to start talking to.

10. *At the end of the party* say goodbye to each guest at the front door. If possible, leave what you are doing and walk to the door with her. Thank her again if she brought you a gift. It's childish to yell, "So long!" from another part of the house to a departing guest.

11. *Thank your parents* for letting you have the party, and, before you collapse, help clean up the mess any good party makes.

❧❀❧

Put More Fun
in
Your Parties

When everything your mother has planned for your party gives out, be ready with a few sure-fire games like these.

Spider web

Each guest is given the end of a string which you have wound throughout the house from basement to attic, indoors and out. All guests start at the same time and the winner is the one who traces his or her string to the end —where a prize is attached to it. Several balls of string and advance preparation are needed as well as cooperation from all family members so "spider webs" won't be disturbed before party time.

Hidden pennies

Hide 100 (or 200, if you feel rich) pennies in the back yard. Again, advance preparation is needed. Winner is the one who finds the most hidden—not buried—pennies. Use

$1.00 or $2.00 of your own allowance and get new pennies at the bank.

Tray of many objects

On a large tray, assemble as many small and different objects as you wish (at least twenty-five)—buttons, kitchen utensils, personal objects, jewelry, sewing equipment, school supplies, tools, little decorative objects from around the house can all be included. Let players study the tray for a given amount of time—usually no longer than ten minutes—then take the tray out of the room, remove four objects, and let each player try to list the four objects that are missing. The winner is the one who correctly names the four missing items first.

Charades

Old as hide-and-seek but a much more sophisticated game. Two teams work secretly in separate rooms, each team writing down six to ten book, movie, or song titles, well-known sayings or advertising slogans, each one printed on a separate slip of paper. The slips are then exchanged between teams. With the teams seated opposite each other, one member at a time is clocked while he or she acts out the words on the paper he has drawn, and while the rest of his team guesses aloud—and frantically—what in the world he's trying to convey with his crazy maneuvers. Team members should work out in advance their own signals for "sounds like," proper names, single or capital letters, foreign country meanings, breakdowns of long words into syllables, etc. A timekeeper tabulates each competitor's time and the winning team is the one with the lower total.

Kooky themes

You don't have to wait for Halloween to dress up for a party. Have a Pirate Party, a Roaring '20s Party, a Caveman–Cave Woman Party, a party to celebrate the first day of spring or summer, to commemorate some historic character, or a Year 2050 Party.

LITTLE TOUCHES THAT ARE REMEMBERED

* Rent an old movie film and a projector to show it after refreshments.

* Have someone photograph everyone at the party with an instant developing camera so people can take the pictures home with them.

* Have a fortune teller, a palm reader, a magician, a card trick expert (professional or amateur).

* Ask each guest to wear something to trade—for keeps.

* Pin a famous name on the back of each guest as he or she arrives, but don't let the guest see the name. During the party guests must speak to each other in ways which give identity clues. The winner is the first person to guess the name of the person he's "wearing." Loser is the last one to catch on.

* Make or buy favors and put one under or beside each guest's place as a surprise when everyone gets to the table. Keep them inexpensive, amusing, useful, or original.

A punch bowl adds glamor to any party

Soft drinks and lemonade are standbys for most parties, but even they should be prepared in advance and put on a separate table or bar along with glasses, ice cubes in a bucket, and napkins. You can serve a fruit punch in a punch bowl to make the party special and to be more formal. Of course, you need to have the bowl and the cups on hand, but they are fairly inexpensive now in many stores and make a great impression, especially at holiday parties. Here are some recipes for fruit punch.

FRUIT AND GINGER ALE PUNCH

1 can (6-ounce size) frozen orange juice
1 can (6-ounce size) frozen lemonade
1 can (6-ounce size) frozen limeade
4 cups cold water
Block of ice or ice cubes
1 large bottle (about 4 cups) ginger ale

Combine all ingredients except ginger ale. Pour over ice block in punch bowl or ice cubes in large pitcher. Add ginger ale just before serving. Makes 12 to 15 punch cups.

CRANBERRY PUNCH

2 pint bottles cranberry juice cocktail
1 quart apple juice
1 can (6-ounce size) frozen lemonade
1 can (6-ounce size) frozen grapefruit juice
1 can (6-ounce size) frozen pineapple juice
Block of ice or ice cubes
2 bottles (29-ounce size) carbonated soda water
12 orange slices, halved

Have all ingredients chilled. Pour juices over block of ice in punch bowl or over ice cubes in glass pitchers. Add carbonated soda water. Stir gently, just enough to mix. Add orange slices. Serve at once. Makes 24 or more punch cups.

SUPER PUNCH WITH SHERBET AND FRESH FRUIT

2 bananas
1 peach
1 cup seedless grapes
1 medium-sized can sliced or chunk pineapple
3 tablespoons honey
1 pint fruit sherbet
2 cups Hawaiian Punch
4 ice cubes

In a blender put 2 bananas, 1 peeled peach (pit removed), a cup of seedless grapes, a medium-sized can of pineapple, 3 tablespoons honey, a pint of raspberry, strawberry, or mixed-flavor sherbet, 2 cups Hawaiian Punch, and 4 ice cubes. Blend them together—in two batches if your blender is small. The crushed ice cubes will make a frothy mixture. Then add enough water to dilute to taste you like. Pour over ice block in punch bowl. When you're over 18, this recipe is delicious with rum added.

NOTE: To make ice block, rinse a half-gallon-sized milk container, fill with water, and freeze. Then peel off cardboard container and slip block into punch bowl. Ice cubes melt too fast in a punch bowl and dilute the flavor.

To serve and sip punch

Arrange the punch bowl, its ladle, and cups on a separate table apart from the rest of the food. It's nice to sprinkle a few leaves or fresh flowers around the base of the bowl and to add candles if your party is in the evening. Lighted candles are never used on tables during luncheon or daytime parties.

A hostess serves punch to her guests and boys serve punch to girls. The method: pick up a cup with your left hand, leaving your right hand free to ladle the punch into the cup. Fill the cup only two thirds full, never to the very rim of the cup. Replace the ladle in the punch bowl. With the filled cup still in your left hand, reach for a napkin and place the cup on the napkin, resting both in the palm of your right hand. To hand a cup to a guest, place your thumb and first finger around the middle of the cup so that you can pass it to your guest with the handle facing her. When you serve yourself, pour the same way, sip, and neatly place the cup on the napkin in your left hand so that the napkin will absorb any spilling that occurs as you walk around. Never stand around a punch bowl too long. Move back so that others can get to it.

A FEW INSIDE TIPS ABOUT PARTYING

* *After a big party* or a special-occasion dinner, thank your hostess by phone or letter, especially if you know she went to considerable trouble and the party involved heavy planning, decorating, and favors.

* *When there's a guest of honor* at a party, all guests are supposed to stay until he or she leaves, providing, of course, the honored person is *not* a house guest.

* *When you have to refuse a party invitation* say you're sorry you can't come, mention why if it seems appropriate, but don't go into detailed explanations about why you aren't free. Don't say, "I'll think about it," "I guess so," or "I don't care," when someone asks you (unless there is a reason to check out another appointment and you intend to let your friend know).

* *Music for dancing* is a great idea for parties. Roll back the rugs, scatter dance wax (any hardware store sells it) or even plain old cornmeal on the floor, see that tapes,

records, and players are in working order, and have a ball. But if there's going to be loud music, tip off your neighbors in advance, and give them the approximate time when they can take the cotton out of their ears.

Toasts

Girls and women rarely make toasts, but it's good to know a little about them. Toasting another person is the highest honor you can pay him. When everyone at a dinner raises a glass (in your case Coke; later on it will be wine) and says "Cheers" or "To your health," it conveys special warmth and praise. Every nation has its toast. The French say "Bon Santé" (good health), the Scandinavians say "Skoal," the Israelis say "L'Chaim," and in pubs all over England they say, "'Ere's mud in your eye." In fact, early England gave us the word "toast." Sitting around an open fire, men dropped a piece of toasted bread into a glass of wine, then drank until the glass was empty of everything except the little piece of toast—it meant they were friends to the end. Also in those days they smashed their glasses on the stones of the fireplace after they'd toasted a woman or a very special person—to prevent the glass from ever being used again for less sacred reasons.

Even though we don't smash glasses today, toasts are important. The person making the toast to his host or hostess or to the guest of honor rises to his feet and, with his glass in his hand, says something nice about the person being toasted, ending with, "And therefore I propose a toast to the greatest party giver in Georgetown." Then he raises his glass to eye level, waits for others to stand, and all sip a little wine.

The only time you don't join in a toast is when you are

the one being toasted. Then you sit there and blush. When the toast is over, everyone sits down, the person being toasted either nods as a thank-you or stands up and says a few words of thanks. If you are the one being toasted, you don't drink from your own glass until all the others have done so, or you'd be drinking to yourself.

It's rude *not* to join in a toast at all; so if you don't want to drink, at least raise the glass to your lips and pretend. There's an old superstition that it's bad luck to toast a person with water, but everything else is fine: orange juice, milk, even iced tea.

Girls and women never rise after they've been toasted unless they're going to make a speech in answer. They just smile their prettiest. Sometimes at a dinner a toast will be made to the President of the United States even though he isn't there. In that case, it will always be the first toast of the evening.

Party Ideas
with
a Different Twist

You can pull together smaller, spur-of-the-moment parties when you'd like something different to do on a lazy summer day, over a rainy weekend, or on a Friday night when nothing seems to be happening. Here are some ideas that are easy, informal, and inexpensive.

TEACH-A-TALENT PARTY

If you know how to do something, invite a small group of your pals to your house and teach them your specialty. No one can be an expert in every creative field, but every girl should develop at least one skill with her hands. You and your friends can take turns being teacher at each other's houses, and, who knows, you might learn to do or make something you thought impossible before. Always choose a night convenient to your mother so she will be free to help you set up the work space, prepare light refreshments, and be on hand to help.

Some things everyone likes to be good at:

Making macrame (pronounced mack-rah-may) belts

Tell each of your friends to bring her own materials—a ball of ecru-colored string and four long nails which will be pounded into a piece of wooden board you (or your brother or father) should supply in case your friends ask too many questions about thickness, size, etc. Once everyone is set up for action, you teach step-by-step until they all get the hang of making their first macrame belts.

Learning to crochet or knit

Every girl should know how to knit and/or crochet. They're both very rewarding pastimes, and although the first attempts may all end up being mile-long scarves, eventually every girl can tackle really beautiful sweaters, afghans, dog sweaters, and gift items that will be cherished. Don't try to teach knitting and crocheting the same evening, but whichever you decide upon, tell each of your friends to bring her own yarn, knitting needles or, in the case of a crochet lesson, her own crochet hook and thread. The younger your friends are, the bigger knitting needles they should buy because they'll produce a lot of knitting in a hurry!

Making silver jewelry

Like stained-glass work, this is an expensive hobby, but everyone loves to watch and learn. So if this is your talent, invite a group for a demonstration. If any of them want to take it up, you can advise on cost, material, places to buy, tools, and tricks of the trade.

Framing favorite photos and paintings or drawings

Hobby shops now sell inexpensive framing kits, so tell your friends to bring along whatever photographs or art work they want to frame for their own rooms or for gifts; then set up a large worktable with scissors, rulers, Scotch tape, etc. Before the evening is over you'll all have your Christmas shopping done.

Drying flowers

Tell each girl to bring one or two thick books (telephone directories or mail order catalogues) and whatever flowers or leaves they love. Caution them to bring single-petal flowers like daisies or violets or field flowers—not thick flowers like marigolds or roses or peonies, which don't dry well. Buttercups, Queen Anne's lace, dainty ferns are beautiful when dried. Flatten the flowers or leaves between pages of the directory, never overlapping one flower onto another. Then leave for at least four or five days to dry after you've piled some heavy books on top for extra pressure. The temptation to peek is strong, so if you do, don't disturb the flowers—just admire and close them back in the book for the necessary drying time. When dry, paste the dried beauties on cards or note sheets, using Elmer's glue diluted with water to avoid lumpiness. Or frame them as gifts after you've pasted them on felt, cardboard, or construction paper.

Making "apple people"

Everyone should be warned that "little old apple people" are created by shrinking real apples—and the shrinkage is surprising—so choose apples three to four inches in di-

166

ameter. When finished they will be no larger than a Ping-Pong ball. Peel the apples, put them on a cookie sheet and bake them in a slow 200-degree oven for four or five hours, or until they've shrunk to the size you want to work with. While they're still warm and soft, mold each apple into the shape of a head. You'll be amazed at how much the apple texture resembles a happy old man's or woman's skin! Next, complete the head using cloves for eyes, cotton fuzz for hair (or if you don't want white hair, cut a nylon stocking right through the middle and unravel it until it resembles black, brown, gray, even red fuzzy hair). To complete the figure, use pipe cleaners for arms, 9-inch styrofoam cones (bought in any hobby shop) for the body—just poke the point of the cone up into the head—and dress the way you would any little doll.

Decorating with stones and pebbles

Tell your friends to gather small stones or pebbles, and to bring along any empty cans, jars, or bottles they want to decorate. Using Elmer's glue, cover entire outside with stones, then wait one week for glue to dry before spraying with clear lacquer (if you spray too soon you will loosen all the stones). Hints for gifts: pebble-covered tuna cans are perfect to hold stamps on Dad's desk, empty tomato paste cans (small-sized) for paper clips, empty spice or mustard jars to hold pencils or Mom's various make-up brushes, etc.

Making "stone-age" people

These are wonderful gifts and house ornaments. Select stones with a nice shape—at least one should resemble a face—and, using full-strength Elmer's glue, attach head, body, arms together, then glue them onto the flattest base stone you have. Paint them with any interior paint you have, spray with clear lacquer when paint is dry. As in "apple people" you can use sequins, buttons, beads, little gold loops from broken earrings—anything you find around the house—to make a "stone person" come to life.

Learning to use a sewing machine

If you're good at using a sewing machine, threading it, changing bobbins, etc., it means you're talented in a most useful way; so invite those friends who also have access to machines to come to your house for a basic beginner's lesson. Show them how to cut a simple pattern and stitch it up. It will banish their fear of a remarkable machine that can bring out lots of creativity in girls who have more fashion sense than money. Later on, several of you can gather at one house to work together, now that most sewing machines are lighter and more portable than a stack of school books.

A PROGRESSIVE DINNER PARTY

It takes a little planning, but a progressive dinner is a whole afternoon and evening of fun. Each friend is assigned one course to be served and eaten at her house, and the whole gang goes from house to house until all courses have been devoured, starting with a fruit cup, for example, through a main course, salad, bread and butter with something "extra" like cheese, to dessert. Amounts to a lot of food but you walk it all off between courses and houses.

A "COME AS YOU ARE" PARTY

This one must be done on the spur of the moment and must

include close friends who will really come dressed as they are when you telephone: if they've been washing their hair, they come in a towel; if they've been painting their bikes, they come in messy jeans still dripping with enamel; if they've been having a dress re-hemmed, they come with the pins still hanging there. Important: no cheating, and you'll be able to check this by the time elapsed between telephone invitation and your friend's appearance at the door.

A "SLOW-DANCE" PRACTICE PARTY

Try this only if you've got an older brother or sister who is willing to teach your friends to slow-dance and suffer bruised ankles and toes until they get the hang of it. Invite both boys and girls and, if you don't have the right records, tell some of them to bring a few favorites along. Serve Cokes and cookies when the going gets tough.

A BREAD-BAKING PARTY

You supply the know-how and all the ingredients, then invite some friends over for an afternoon's fun of watching you (and taking notes) make bread. Let your friends do some of the measuring, sifting, kneading—as a reward they get to eat hot, buttery home-made bread straight from the oven. All cookbooks have dependable recipes, but here is one that is special because it requires no long waiting, no kneading at all.

CUBAN BREAD

(A quick and easy French bread by one of the best chefs in the world, James Beard):

1 package or 1 cake yeast
2 cups lukewarm water
1¼ tablespoons salt
1 tablespoon sugar
6 to 9 cups regular flour

DIRECTIONS:

Dissolve the yeast in the warm water and add the salt and sugar, stirring thoroughly. Add the flour a cup at a time, beating it in with a wooden spoon, adding enough flour to make a smooth dough. When dough is well mixed, cover it with a towel, put it in a warm place (near a warm stove or on a table in front of a sunny window), and let it rise until it's double in size. Then put the dough on a lightly floured surface and shape it into long, French-style loaves or round, Italian-style loaves or small, individual loaves. Arrange these on a cookie sheet heavily sprinkled with cornmeal.

Allow to rise 5 minutes more. Then slash the tops with a knife in two or three places, brush them with water and place them in a COLD oven. Set the oven for 400 degrees and start it. Add a pan of boiling water to the oven (to make necessary moist air for best baking results) and bake the loaves until crusty and done. About 40 to 45 minutes for regular-size loaves.

NOTE: You can also add sesame or poppy seeds. Sprinkle them on top just before you pop the bread into the oven.

"I Don't Have Anything...
(deep sigh)...
to Do!"

Sometimes you can barely wait until you're old enough to jump in a car and just drive off to a friend's house, a movie, or even to the local jeanery for some new pants. But for the most part when you want to go somewhere you're still a victim of your parents' schedules, so that means plenty of spare time on your hands. Well, use it to develop your best talents, not only for your own pleasure but in pursuits that will also give pleasure to others. Here are some ideas for birthday or Christmas gifts you can make as well as other fun activities.

Make candles

Molds, special wax, and colorings are inexpensive and available at hobby stores or from mail order catalogs.

Sew

Use basic one-step patterns (every pattern book now has a special section of simplified patterns for the beginner,

including easy-to-make blouses, wrap skirts, smocks, aprons, and sports accessories). And sewing machines are now geared for beginners, with such helpful gadgets as self-winding bobbins and automatic needle-threaders. Wherever you rent or buy a sewing machine, you can have free lessons. Or if you already have a machine, you can enroll in sewing classes; often they are free.

Crochet, knit, spool-knit

At many yarn shops you will receive a basic lesson in simple knitting or crocheting for the price of the yarn or thread. Start with a scarf, a small blanket, or a cover you can sew for a lounge pillow or bed pillow. You can even knit or crochet while you listen to, or 90-percent-watch, television.

Paint decorative designs on ordinary clay garden pots or coffee containers

Use waterproof acrylics or enamels, then fill them with inexpensive plants from the dime store for gifts or for your own room.

Embroider

Use jeans, T-shirts, smocks, or old-fashioned night-gowns you will find if you shop the used-clothing stores or antique shops. Draw your own designs or buy transfers from a sewing shop or the notions department of your local store.

Learn to refinish small pieces of furniture from junk shops or garage sales

Every paint store now sells antique-ing sets or kits with new wet-look modern effects. Start with a small bookcase, a foot stool, a shelf for miniatures, a mirror with an unusual frame. Modernize it or make it look even more ancient than it is.

Make a store-all

Attend neighborhood garage sales or scour second-hand stores until you find an old trunk. Line it with bright printed or striped cotton, clean up and varnish the exterior, and use it for your record albums, tapes, scrapbooks, or any of your favorite possessions, such as the plush toys you've hung on to since childhood.

Learn to cook

You can use regular cookbooks now, and your mother can help you select foolproof recipes for cookies, cakes, brownies, pancakes from scratch. When you've clocked up a few hours in the kitchen, you can go on to bread making; there are now a number of cookbooks devoted only to recipes for breads. Most of them require patience and lots of time because you must wait for breads to rise at least once, then you have to knead the dough.

Be a pet-keeper

Gerbils are the cleanest and require only an old aquarium, some cedar chips, and an exercise wheel for them to play on. After gerbils and other pet shop rodents, you'll soon find yourself graduating to more exotic animals and birds, though we don't recommend reptiles unless you have unusually calm parents.

Make scrapbooks and photo albums to keep forever

If you can't find enough photos around the house, ask for an inexpensive camera for your next birthday and start taking pictures yourself. Everything you put in an album while you're still pre-teenage will be worth its weight in gold when you're older. Like fine wine, the older it gets the more cherished it is.

Learn to use carpenter tools

Build a bird house, a pet or dog house, boxes with latches and hinges (buy them at any hardware store) for your cassettes and tapes.

Make your own doll house

Collect miniature furniture and accessories, then design a house worthy of them. Plan it on paper, find a wooden crate from which you can remove the fourth side, and use the top of the crate for the "second floor." Make partitions of thin wood or heavy posterboard. Then decorate interior walls with paint or wallpaper samples and hang miniature mirrors and picture frames on them. Cover floors with sample tiles or pieces of old carpeting. You can create tiny furnishings or buy them in toy stores or antique markets.

Be a car washer-and-polisher for fun and profit

Ask your parents to underwrite the cost of your basic supplies in return for one month's free wash, polish, and inside clean-up. Then broaden your Saturday morning enterprise by soliciting business from neighbors with dusty specimens parked in their driveways.

Grow herbs in clay pots

Select seeds of chives, parsley, basil, bay leaf, tarragon, marjoram in the local garden shop or hardware store, follow planting directions, and when herbs are growing nicely, sell them to neighbors or at school charity bazaars. This idea works best in fall and winter when people can't grow herbs in their own gardens.

How to Conduct Meetings

If you want to start a club of your own, you can do so with just a few friends (then everyone can be an officer with a title) who want to do things together for fun, money-raising, or a charitable community cause. From Girl Scout or 4-H clubs to national political conventions, the basic rules for conducting a meeting are pretty much the same. Here's the way to do it.

Elected officers

THE PRESIDENT is the most important officer because she presides over all meetings, appoints special committees, and signs all papers for the club.

THE VICE-PRESIDENT is second in importance and takes over when the President isn't there.

THE SECRETARY keeps "minutes" of each meeting—brief notes of what was discussed, planned, argued about, and finally decided.

THE TREASURER keeps track of the club's dues, earnings from any bazaar or garage sale, special money gifts. She actually *keeps* the money (separate from her own) in a piggy bank or her own savings account and has a written account of it in a notebook for all club members to check during meetings. It is important to keep track of all club funds in a systematic way if you are the Treasurer, because the money you are handling is not your own.

Terms to know if you conduct meetings

ADJOURN—to close a meeting until the next time.

ADOPT—to accept a "motion" or suggestion after the club members have voted on it and a majority has voted Yes.

AGENDA—a list of things to be done or discussed during a meeting.

AMEND—to change the wording of a motion.

AYE and NAY—Aye (pronounced "I") means YES; Nay means NO—words to express your sentiments when there is a voice vote rather than a written ballot.

BALLOT—any sheet of paper used for secret voting.

CALL TO ORDER—the words the President uses to open the meeting.

THE CHAIR—the title for whoever is conducting the meeting, usually the President.

CHAIRPERSON—(formerly called Chairman, but no more)—the name for the person in charge of any committee.

COMMITTEE—any group assigned to do a special job for the club.

FLOOR—used to mean the area where the speaker stood. In modern times it means the right to speak: "Jane has the floor. . . ."

MAJORITY—more than half the votes.

MINORITY—any number less than a majority.

177

MINUTES—the written record of what went on during the meeting, including names of those who spoke and topics discussed, measures adopted.

MOTION—a suggestion for acting on a matter: "I make a motion that we have a May Day basket contest. . . ."

NOMINATION—to propose the name of someone for election to an office.

QUORUM—a majority of members present. This is important when a big issue is up for consideration so that one or two members can't put something over on the rest of the members who are away at camp, for example.

RECOGNIZE—a word used by the President or Chairperson to tell a member she has the right to speak: "The Chair recognizes Martha, who will give her opinion about our Christmas budget. . . ."

SECOND—to support or back up a suggestion: "I second the motion that we have an all-night hike. . . ." A motion must be seconded before voting on it can begin.

How a meeting operates

1. *The call to order.* The President or the Chairperson raps a gavel on the desk and says, "The meeting will please come to order."

2. *Roll Call.* All attendance is checked; this is also the time to welcome new members or guests.

3. *Reading of the Minutes.* The President asks the Secretary to do so. Then the President asks for someone to make a motion that the minutes as read are correct; after the motion a "seconding" is asked for. Then a vote is taken to accept the minutes.

4. *Treasurer's Report.* The President asks the Treasurer to report on the club's finances. No motion is possible because only the Treasurer knows the facts.

5. *Special Committee Reports.* The President asks the Chair-person or head of any committee to tell what is happening with her project.
6. *New Business.* The President, or any member, can bring up subjects, projects, or problems as "new business" for all members to discuss and vote on.
7. *Program.* If there is any entertainment or a special speaker is scheduled, it is introduced by the President or the head of the committee arranging the event.
8. *Announcements.* The President or Chair announces the date, time, and place of the next meeting.
9. *Adjournment.* The President or Chair says, "If there is no further business, this meeting is adjourned." No motion is needed.

Some important committees

THE NOMINATING COMMITTEE decides which members will be proposed as potential officers the club will elect.

THE PUBLICITY COMMITTEE is in charge of signs, posters, announcements to the public, the school, the neighborhood for all special club events.

THE FINANCE COMMITTEE collects dues and thinks up ways to make money for the club's activities, club house, special charity.

THE PROGRAM COMMITTEE is in charge of club parties, guest speakers, special entertainment, or events to keep the club alive and to attract new members.

Manners
for Boys Only

Many of the old formalities concerning "ladies and gentle-men" have either disappeared completely or become easy-going personal choices. Girls wear boys' jeans, participate in sports with boys on an equal basis, study for careers that used to be For Men Only. But some manners don't change because they're still useful and helpful when girls and boys start going places together. Fathers and big brothers usually tell boys what is expected of them as they step out into the social world, but sometimes a boy forgets or is timid, so it's good for girls to know some of the rules. When a girl waits for a boy to open a door for her, smiling as if she has always had *all* doors opened for her, it's a lot easier for him to do the right thing: step forward, open the door with a flourish, and feel ten feet tall as the girl precedes him.

Here are some other things boys are expected to do:

1. *Boys walk on the curb side of the street,* whether it's with one girl, two, or three. When two boys are walking with one girl, the girl walks in the middle. If the girl stops to talk with a friend on the street, the boy walks on slowly—the

girl will call him back quickly if she knows the person well enough to make an introduction.

2. *Boys let women and girls go first* whenever it's physically possible. Here are the exceptions:

   * In a place of worship, unless there is an usher, the boy leads the way and finds a place to sit. Then he stands with his back to the altar and lets the girl enter the pew first.

   * In a restaurant or theater where there is no waiter or usher to show people to their places, the boy goes first to find a table or a seat. In a crowd, the boy goes ahead of the girl to clear the way.

   * When leaving a bus, train, or subway, the boy gets off first to help the girl out. He stands just outside the door to give her a hand if the doors start to close. In elevators, men and boys stand back until all women have left the elevator.

   * When getting into a taxi, the boy opens the door and says to the girl, "I'll get in first so you won't have to slide over." Then, when she's in, he reaches over and pulls the door shut. This is particularly comforting when a girl is wearing a long dress.

3. *Boys open doors for women.* The technique is this: The boy moves ahead of the girl quickly to get near the door, pulls it open, then steps back to let her walk through. If it's a revolving door, the boy pushes the door to an open space and holds it there for her to enter.

4. *Boys help women and girls put on their coats.* He holds the girl's coat open, a little below shoulder height (hers, not his), then he keeps it steady so that she can aim first one

arm, then the other, into the sleeves. A boy helps a girl take off her coat by stepping behind her and waiting for the crucial moment when the coat begins to slide off her shoulders. Then he takes it with both hands.

5. *Boys remove their hats* the moment they step into a house, a school, a church (but not a synagogue), a theater, a restaurant, an elevator, when the American flag goes by, when the National Anthem is being sung or played, and when standing on the street talking to a girl or woman. He holds his hat, puts it down, or checks it, but doesn't put it back on until he's leaving.

6. *A boy always asks his party hostess for a dance* during the evening; and at a dinner-dance the two women between whom he sat during dinner. One dance each will do; the rest of the evening his responsibility is toward the girl he brought to the dance.

7. *A boy calls for a girl at her home* by ringing the doorbell, entering the house, and greeting some member of the girl's family if only to say, "How do you do?" and shake hands. Usually, the girl's parents will make it clear to the boy when the girl is expected home—a decision that has probably been discussed before he arrives so there is very little he can do to change it.

8. *A boy lets a girl go ahead of him* when they go down the receiving line at a big party or dance. Both greet the host and hostess, or the chaperones, shake hands, say at least one sentence pertaining to the evening ("The decorations are terrific," or "This is my favorite band.") and then move on. They must not stand and tell a long story. Before leaving the party, the boy leads the girl over to say goodnight and thank you to the same hostess, host, or chaperones.

Final Word

There are much harder things to do
than simply growing up
or growing up simply,
but I can't think of any myself,
so I say pay attention to the world
inside and outside of you,
don't worry about tomorrow or yesterday or even
what's happening today; try to have fun.

ANN BUCHWALD

If Your Birthday is	Your Zodiac Sign is
December 21 – January 19	<u>Capricorn</u> (May be overcritical of others... but capable of reaching highest goals herself)
January 20 – February 18	<u>Aquarius</u> (May be too much of a dreamer ... but always an honest individualist)
February 19 – March 20	<u>Pisces</u> (May withdraw into her shell... but intuitively knows how to help others)
March 21 – April 20	<u>Aries</u> (May seem bossy because she's so inspiring and inventive)
April 21 – May 20	<u>Taurus</u> (May be a bit stubborn ..., but what tenacity and dependability!)
May 21 – June 20	<u>Gemini</u> (May try to do too many things at once ... because she's bright and quick witted)
June 21 – July 20	<u>Cancer</u> (May cry when small things go wrong... because she loves the whole world and hates suffering)
July 21 – August 21	<u>Leo</u> (May seem arrogant... because she's a born leader)
August 22 – September 22	<u>Virgo</u> (May quibble with others over how things should be done ... she's a perfectionist herself)
September 23 – October 22	<u>Libra</u> (May be an escapist because she loves harmony and balance so much)
October 23 – November 22	<u>Scorpio</u> (May be hypersensitive... because she's courageous on the outside, tender on the inside)
November 23 – December 20	<u>Sagittarius</u> (May take too many risks... but everybody trusts and admires her)